CW00542686

corner plates

T

Sleepy Quainton Road, in the 1930s, attractively surrounded by the 'Metroland'
green open fields would have Brill, it was once reached, its Metropolitan 'Metropolitan' the patient
suburbia train to mixed; assembly of foreground, is the 41 at the
branch of a typically interest. The long 'S.C.' hoped in sight No. 41 at the
head. Of particular area. The of wagons on Clarke), coal
coach. in the familiar initials could Neasden been greenish-grey with maroon
platform once many wagons could Neasden the far sidings
carry, whose yard at have been generating station.
factors, the locomotive is believed to maroon
including colour scheme is believed to

London London Transport Executive

THE BRILL TRAMWAY

Including the Railway
from Aylesbury to
Verney Junction

Bill Simpson

Oxford Publishing Co.

Copyright © 1985 Oxford Publishing Co.

ISBN 0-86093-218-4

All rights reserved. No part of this book may be reproduced or transmitted in any form or by any means, electronic or mechanical, including photocopying, recording or any information storage and retrieval system, without permission in writing from the Publisher.

ACKNOWLEDGEMENTS

The author would like to express his gratitude to the following people and institutions:

Special thanks go to Mike Crosbie who researched exhaustively to compile the many drawings of installations along the Brill line and the line to Verney Junction, plus much more additional material. Thanks also go to Councillor Bill George of Grendon Underwood for establishing many personal contacts in the area of the book. To Messrs Jack Roberts, Tom Rolfe, the late Stan Pointer, Jack Bunyan, Mrs Brown, Annie Kirby, Harry Reed, Mrs Gilbert, Mrs Young, Tom Wallington, W. E. Fenemore, Mrs Rowley, David Evans, Mrs M. E. Washington, Mrs Busby, Mrs Brunner of Wotton House, Bill Fry, Jack Turner, Andrew Emmerson, Alan Vessey of the Quainton Railway Preservation Society, The London Underground Society, Mike Horne, Martin Byles, Roy Slaymaker, R. C. Riley, John Pritchett, L. Harding, and to my wife, De, who worked on the research and did the final typing of the manuscript.

My thanks also go to these essential sources without which no work could be compiled in detail, matched by the patience and cordiality of the helpful staff: Aylesbury County Library (Buckingham Collection, Ruth Watts), Aylesbury Museum (Mr Gowing and Miss L Babbs), Aylesbury Record Office, Buckingham Library, Oxford Record Office (Miss Barnes), Greater London County Council Record Office, Public Record Office, Kew, and The Swindon Railway Museum.

BIBLIOGRAPHY

The Duke of Buckingham's Railways by Charles E. Lee, Railway Magazine, October 1935
The Aylesbury & Buckingham Railway by W. E. Edwards, The Railway Magazine, 1908
The Met. Tanks by Brien Reed, Loco Profile No. 10
The Wotton Tramway by Ken Jones, Oakwood Press
Metropolitan Steam by E. J. S. Gadsden, Roundhouse Books
The Oxford & Aylesbury Tram Road by F. Goodman, The Railway Magazine, 1899
The Railway Observer
Temple Estate Collection, Aylesbury Record Office
The Chandos Papers, The London Underground Society
The Buckingham Express
The Bucks Herald
Board of Trade Report dated 20th July 1873 by Col. Yolland
Board of Trade Report dated 19th October 1894 by General C. S. Hutchinson
Board of Trade Report dated 11th November 1911 by Col. Von Donop

Typesetting by:
Aquarius Typesetting Services, New Milton, Hants.

Printed in Great Britain by:
William Clowes Ltd., Beccles, Suffolk.

Published by:
Oxford Publishing Co.
Link House
West Street
POOLE, Dorset

PREFACE

One can be very easily distracted by the residual charm of the Brill Tramway. In many ways the endearment of the line so perfectly fills the imagined ideal of the country railway. It is an endearment that belies some hard realities in its past.

The aristocrat that built the line did so to advantage the economy of his estates, to draw together the strands of erstwhile production in dairy produce, animal and arable agriculture and the considerable demand for bricks, tiles and timber. It brought into the estate a supply of coal, livestock for fattening, ale, manure and chalk for the land. With a view to greater prosperity the Duke tried, unsuccessfully, to have the line recognised as a proper railway by the Board of Trade. This was to precede the heady prospect of the railway being extended to Oxford and becoming a fast Varsity-Metropolis link developing as part of early commuter railways; an optimistic prospect that unfortunately for its promoters did not find enough support elsewhere.

When construction of the line commenced, the measure of jubilation in the neighbourhood, not for the trade benefits, but the opportunity of full employment during the coming winter, reflects the foreboding of the agrarian household for the onset of that season.

Although only a short line, little more than six miles in length, the Brill Tramway could not have been an easy line to work. Early locomotives were difficult to operate and had a somewhat chequered success. This was due in part to the permanent way. Being of such light construction, intended originally for horse traction, regular derailments were a source of vexation throughout its working life. There was also sparse protection from the weather for the staff, and the lack of even a simple goods crane at any of the stations must have caused much avoidable handling.

There is, of course, another side to the coin. Many of the countrymen did enjoy a sense of stability working for and alongside the Tramway, which was not the minor concern of some far away headquarters in city offices, for the roots of its identity remained deeply local.

Eventually, after many years, the line was overtaken by alternative routes and the onset of developing road transport. After first being drawn into the expanding net of the Metropolitan Railway, which gave way to the London Transport system, the line lost patronage along with the parent line, the Aylesbury & Buckingham Railway, from which it was a branch. When closure loomed, there was much sympathy, but local regrets tended to be palliated with greater humour than a sense of loss. That was in 1935, when there were still plenty of railways.

Fifty years later, it can be seen as the first withering of the vulnerable short strands; dissolution that would drastically reduce a transport system once so diverse that one could, in comparative comfort, span the distance between such sleepy outposts as Brill and Verney Junction to the heart of the busiest of capitals in but a few hours.

Bill Simpson
Banbury
1985

Due to revision to this survey of 1872-85, a number of anachronisms tend to confuse. With a few exceptions, the period is about 1926, the Kingswood branch now being termed 'disused'. Following the line from Quainton Road, where the replacement of the crossing with a bridge is clearly evident, the train would soon be at the first of the five road crossings on the line. This is where the Waddesdon to Claydon country lane crosses on its rambling path. Waddesdon Station is situated at the junction of the Quainton Road and Bicester to Aylesbury Road (Akeman Street). The line crosses this road and begins its diverting path from the roadside and through the open fields to the next station of Westcott. As it does, so it passes beneath the gallic turrets of Waddesdon Manor, secretive in an enclave of trees. At the village road of Westcott is the second station, the junction for the thread of a long siding to the Waddesdon Estate gasworks. Crossing over the road, the branch has its longest section through the farmland without station or crossing, before it curves into the important pause of Wotton Station, after passing beneath the bridge of the GWR & GCR Joint line; a product of the warring personalities of the Metropolitan and Great Central Railway. After Wotton, there is the much longer branch from a branch to the Kingswood Lane coal wharf; this diverts off to the right.

The line to Brill continues west, passing its closest point to the line's progenitor, the home of the Duke of Buckingham, Wotton House. One of the house driveways is crossed on the level near the Dorton to Brill Road at a familiar spot known as Thame Lodge. As the railway kinks alongside the road, it enters the echoing green of ancient Rushbeds Wood, and within the wood is the appropriately named Wood Siding Station. Although it is the remotest station on the Brill line, after 1910 it was virtually perched above the thundering express trains of the GWR, and the crimson Metropolitan locomotive could be seen in the same view as the Brunswick green of 'Castles' and 'Kings' running between Paddington and Birmingham. Continuing through the wood, until reaching the open climb through a shallow cutting, on a reverse curve, the train would reach its terminus at Brill. There would still be quite a walk for passengers to the village which was situated on high. Between roads to Ludgershall, that pass by the station, and another towards Muswell Hill, can be seen the dozen or so tiny specks of the buildings of small brickworks that so industriously scarred the hillside with their workings.

Ordnance Survey

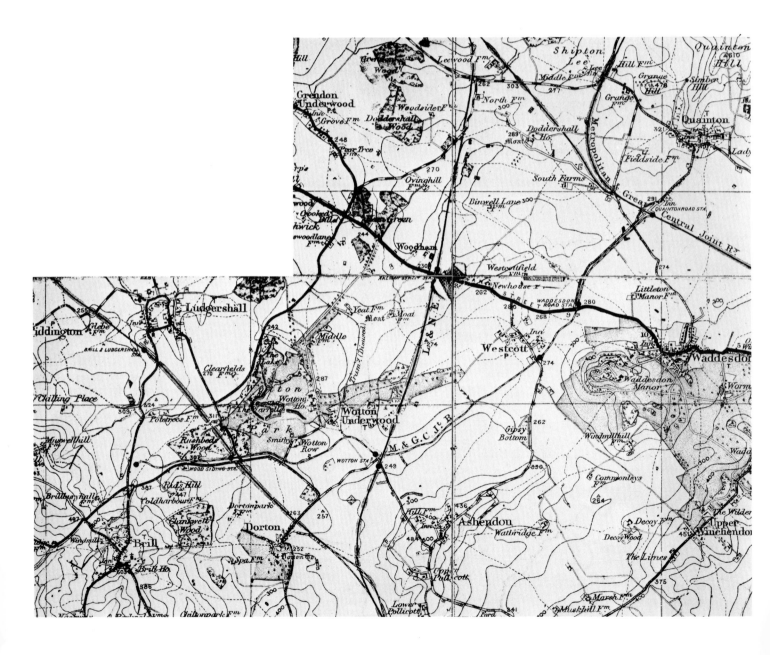

CONTENTS

CHAPTER ONE

The Aylesbury & Buckingham Railway

In April 1872, the village of Brill acquired a railway station. It was not a very big station even by small country branch line standards. Its facilities were frugal in the extreme and with a regulation speed of five miles per hour, for its oddly assembled mixed trains, it could not be regarded as anything more than the most tenuous of railway connections. Nevertheless, in its highly individual form the ancient community of Brill entered the railway age.

Brill, with a population of 1,400, was by far the largest village that this line served. The other villages along the 6¼ mile route from the junction at Quainton were Waddesdon, Westcott and Wotton, but many other villages were able to derive some benefit from the line, especially the farming communities.

The fact that this odd little line was built at all derives from the interest and enthusiasm of the local landowner, the third Duke of Buckingham. Most of the land upon which the line was built was on his estates, with the family home, Wotton House, being close to the site of Wotton Station. The Duke paid for the line and used the labour from his estate during the winter after the harvest work had been completed. By 1872, the Duke's interest in railways was well-known, as he had been energetic in promoting other Buckinghamshire railway schemes and had served as the Chairman of that mighty developing empire, the London & North Western Railway.

The building of estate tramways was not a new idea, as in 1857, Captain Peel, son of the famous statesman Robert Peel, built a line of some three miles in length from the Great Northern Railway station at Sandy in Bedfordshire to serve his estates. Like the Wotton Tramway it had not been intended originally other than anything more than an agricultural line, but it did, under public persuasion, provide a passenger service.

After their opposition to the incursive growth of railways in the early part of the century, the nobility soon begn to realise that the benefits destined to follow rail communication outweighed the forfeiture. Ironically, the Palace of Stowe in Buckingham, home of the third Duke's father and grandfather, had been a powerhouse of obstruction, especially with regard to George and Robert Stephenson's first survey for the London & Birmingham Railway. As Marquess of Chandos, the third Duke succeeded his father's title in 1861.

The origins of the Wotton Tramway, as it was first called, lie beyond the date of 1872, in the more turbulent period of railway speculation and development, 1845-1851. During this period the Duke, along with another prominent local landowner, Sir Harry Verney of Claydon House, near Claydon, Bucks., built up local support to encourage first of all the London & Birmingham Railway and later, when it became part of that great amalgamate, the London & North Western Railway, to build a line from Bletchley to Oxford, with a junction near Claydon for a line branching off to Banbury. Also as part of their plans, they proposed a line from this same junction to run south and join at Aylesbury with the existing line, built from the London & Birmingham main line at Cheddington to that same town. The Bletchley to Oxford lines were really like branches on each side of the junction, with the main line running direct up the centre through Aylesbury, Banbury and on to Birmingham via the GWR. As the junction was to be built on the lands of Sir Harry Verney, it took the name Verney Junction.

However, the southern arm in this grand scheme was to prove something of a contentious issue in the boardroom of the L&NWR, who found favour with all of the plan save this section, which, from their point of view, was superfluous, as the town of Aylesbury was already served by the aforementioned branch from their main line and they could see no advantage in supporting another connection.

It was, in effect, a conflict of motives, the local promoters seeing the lines in terms of long-distance feeders at four compass points, whereas the larger concern saw them as branches from the main line. In 1847 an investment crisis ensured that the southern arm was, in fact, abandoned for the time being. It is very likely that had it been built, the Duke would have built the Tramway earlier.

It was largely due to another local businessman, Mr J. K. Fowler, a chronicler and entrepreneur of Aylesbury, that the old Aylesbury line scheme was regenerated. Mr Fowler mentions in his *Records of Old Times* his conversation with two gentlemen, a Mr Brydone, an engineer from the Great Northern Railway and a Mr F. Rummens, a railway building contractor, who spoke of their plans to propose a line from the Aylesbury terminus of the L&NWR to Oxford. Fowler threw doubts on the success of this proposal, as the GWR had already taken the necessary steps in a recent parliamentary session to cross the Chilterns and reach Oxford via High Wycombe and Thame. He then raised the spectre of the missing section of the through route, between Aylesbury and Verney Junction, as the ideal prospect. Eager to enforce the point, he took the two gentlemen to meet Sir Harry Verney, who saw hope of vindicating the earlier plan along with the Duke of Buckingham and Chandos to whom he urged that the three men should meet straight away. On finding the Duke at home at Wotton, the men were heartened further by his encouragement, with the provision that instead of the line taking the direct route, as formerly planned, through Pitchcott Gap, that it should be diverted a little to the west, closer to Wotton, in fact. The Duke mentioned that he had in mind a small estate tramway branching from the first proposed line and this deviation would allow him to build this almost entirely over his own land.

With the Duke's offer of £5,000 in support, plus acceptance of the chairmanship, not to mention his existing position as Chairman of the L&NWR, the deviation seemed a small concession. The gentlemen were able to withdraw and arrange their future meetings, and with every reason for great optimism, a line as good as made.

However, this Casus Belli of the L&NWR boardroom was not to be resurrected lightly, and the Duke's influence was not able to sway beyond a tacit acceptance by the L&NWR for the agreement to support and work the line when completed.

It was 1860 when the eager promoters had discussed the matter so amicably with the railway powers in the area and, on 6th August of the same year, an Act of Incorporation took place, but it was going to be another eight long and troubled years before the line of 12¾ miles would at last be built and opened on 23rd September 1868.

Before construction work began, the Secretary of the new company, Mr J. G. Rowe, exchanged correspondence with the secretary of the L&NWR, that they would be prepared to work the new railway on 'fair and equitable terms'. It seemed that the Euston boardroom had at last been palliated. Obviously, the fact that the Chairman of both companies was the Duke of Buckingham would prove no little influence in the matter.

Although the line received the Royal Assent on 6th August 1860, and work began from the Claydon end in February 1861, the same year that the Duke left the L&NWR, it passed through an infancy of serious financial storms that matched its earlier conflicts. Initiated on a capital sum of £100,000 divided into 4,000 shares of £25 each, with borrowing powers up to £32,000 proved to be more than optimistic. This had to be modified before presentation to £98,000 in 3,920 shares of £25 each. However, calls on shares became somewhat constrained owing to an investment crisis in 1866, whilst every effort to building delay was exerted by acrimonious landowners, and there was a great deal of compensation haggling.

Delay and reassessment of the work on the line brought about two further Acts, the first on 25th July 1864 to increase the capital by a further £12,000, and another on 19th June of the following year for the enormous sum of £111,000. Clearly there were some anxious moments for the protagonists. The line was under a penalty to be completed in five years, and as it struggled to that end in 1868, with the contractor Mr F. Rummens having to be paid partly in scrip, another blow was struck, which could have been fatal. The L&NWR abandoned the all important link with their line from the Aylesbury Station, even though this was under construction. This volte-face by the larger company must have seemed like an act of treachery in the extreme, exerted by a company that knew the parlous position of the Aylesbury & Buckingham Railway with not a penny, as yet, being earned to offset the large debt. With no trains or staff to earn any, the position must have seemed desperate and it can only be concluded that the logical reason for their behaviour is that it would have been possible to salvage an inevitable bankruptcy at a favourable price. The Duke of Buckingham no longer served on the L&NWR Board, and had now taken up the responsible post of the President of Madras. Furthermore, the interim death of the former Secretary, Stewart, with whom the agreement had been made for the Aylesbury & Buckingham Railway, aided the antagonists. Euston had now become a friendless place.

In such a desperate plight, it can be conjectured that the A&BR looked to a GWR presence in the form of the Wycombe Railway, that arrived in Aylesbury on 1st October 1963 with some relief, even though this was, in fact, a broad gauge line.

After reaching Princes Risborough in 1854, the Wycombe Railway probed a slender finger of the broad gauge to Aylesbury, bringing another front line confrontation in the battle of the gauges. As events proved, this was somewhat fortuitous for the A&BR, who were able to compound a satisfactory agreement with them for a southern outlet; in the Paddington direction.

Third rail conversion of the board gauge, to meet what had become standard gauge, became inevitable. Brunel was dead and even Sir Daniel Gooch could not stem the proliferation of the popular gauge with the GWR in isolation not to extend the broad gauge further. Therefore, the GWR, although seeming to come to the rescue of the small Aylesbury company's plight, were able to extract some advantage from the situation themselves. For with the earliest of conversions undertaken on the Wycombe Railway branch line from Princes Risborough to Aylesbury, the A&BR were to supply one fifth of the cost of conversion of £28,000. The Wycombe Railway itself was absorbed into the GWR in 1867.

After construction of a joint station at Aylesbury, the A&BR were able to conclude a satisfactory arrangement for the hire of trains from the GWR, thus bringing the Swindon profile into the outpost of Verney Junction.

The L&NWR was probably grinding its teeth on the machinations of this resolute little company as they emphasised no through connection facilities at Verney Junction and advertised their own route to Aylesbury with greater vigour, whilst

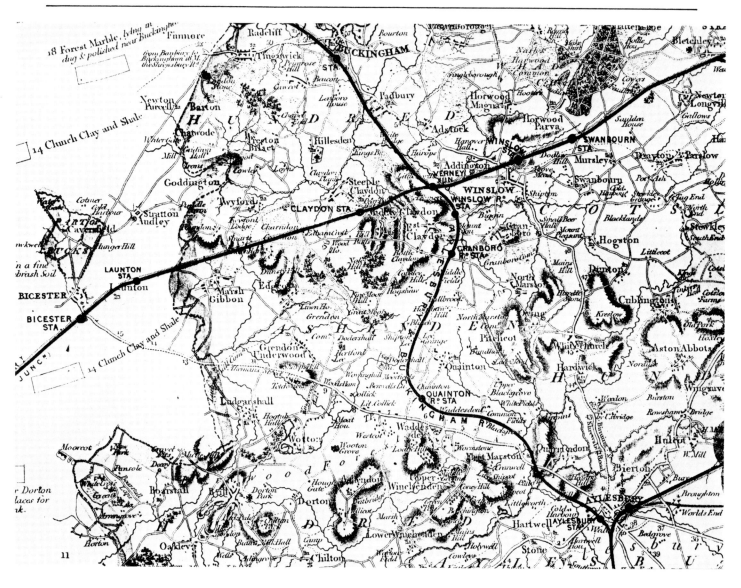

Crutchley's map of the Buckinghamshire district of Aylesbury and Buckingham between 1868 and 1871. Established lines at the top, at Verney Junction, are the east-west line from Bletchley to Oxford, with the branch to Banbury (1850) through Buckingham. The line of the Aylesbury & Buckingham Railway from Aylesbury is clearly delineated with its odd diverting arc to the west, to placate the wishes of the Duke of Buckingham. The original course is drawn with two fine lines through the word 'Pitchcott' — the direct route. The reason for the diversion, the Wotton Tramway, had not by this time been constructed. The distances of stations from Aylesbury became 4¾ miles to the last station to be built (1897), Waddesdon Manor; 6 miles to Quainton Road; 9¾ miles to Grandborough Road; 11 miles to Winslow Road and finally 1¼ miles to Verney Junction. The joining section at Aylesbury, between the London & Birmingham Railway branch of 1839, coming in from the east, and the Wycombe branch of the GWR coming in from the south, implies a connection that did not in fact take place, as the original Aylesbury Station remained an end terminus. However, it is born out of factual intent, as the original agreement between the Aylesbury & Buckingham and the L&NWR, the later proprietors of this line, did include such a link, but into the station, not away from it. It is interesting to survey the remote villages in the area including Brill, Wotton, Grendon Underwood and Ludgershall, eventually to be drawn into the net of the railway communication.

Andrew Emmerson Collection

obstructing the rival line all they could. Posters put up advertising the A&BR Oxford to Bletchley stations were either 'accidentally' covered by obstructions, or pasted over by other posters.

The stations on this little railway were as follows: from the Aylesbury direction; Quainton Road 6 miles, Granborough Road 9¾ miles and Winslow Road 11 miles; a remaining 1¼ miles carried the rails into Verney Junction. Waddesdon Manor Station was opened by the Metropolitan Railway in 1897.

The Great Western Railway supplied the motive power, also first, second and third class carriages. Staff for the train were also in the GWR employ; driver, stoker and guard. The Aylesbury & Buckingham Railway were to supply stationmasters, porters, and any ancillary staff. The trains were rented to the company at a fixed mileage charge of 1s. 1½d. (6p) per mile, resulting in about 13s. 6d. (67½p) per trip for three trips each day. The service comprised three trains each way daily, composed of four wheel carriages.

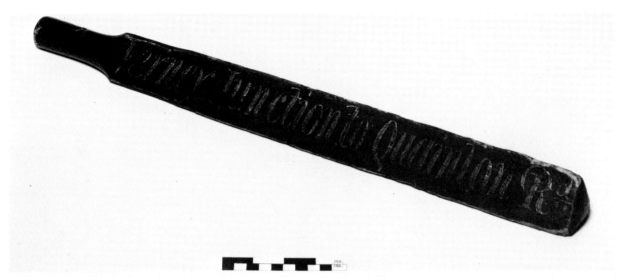

The staff for the original single line working between Aylesbury and Verney Junction. Staff working was in two sections, from Aylesbury to Quainton Road (square-shaped wooden staff) and from Quainton Road to Verney Junction (triangular with the names of the stations painted on in a fine cursive hand).

Buckinghamshire County Museum

Aylesbury Railway Station in 1883; originally a broad gauge terminus of the Wycombe Railway from Maidenhead, High Wycombe and Princes Risborough. It became a through station with the extension north to Verney Junction in 1868. After becoming part of the Metropolitan Railway in 1891, it was expanded further until it was receiving the main line expresses of the GCR in 1899. Of particular note, on this map, beside the small station buildings, is the original broad gauge goods shed, which was closer to the station than the later shed and, on the engine side, is the turntable at the entrance to the shed. This remained as a two road shed until demolition in the 1960s. At the north end of the 'up' platform is the first small signal box. Another much larger box was put in at the south of the station with the arrival of the Metropolitan. The bare 'down' platform would be for the use of the impecunious Aylesbury & Buckingham Railway.

Ordnance Survey

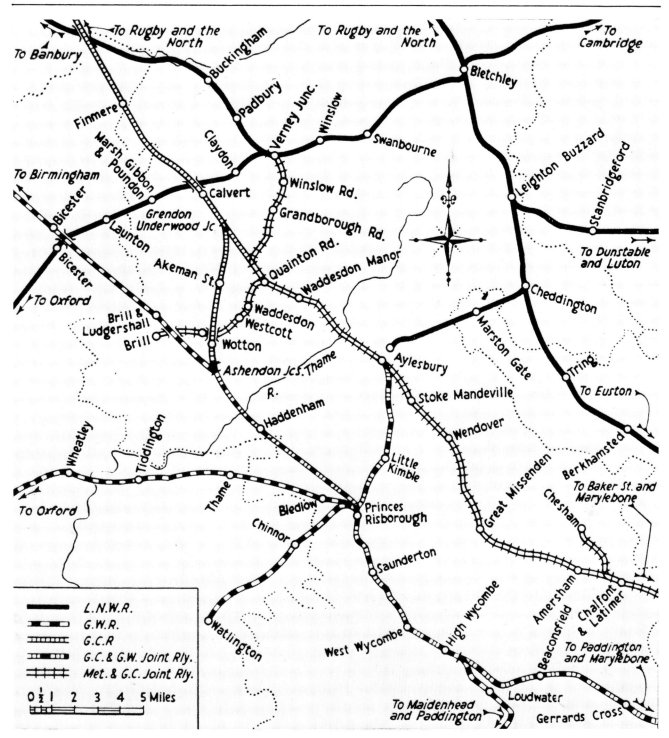

A general view of railway development in the area at its zenith; 1935.
Railway Magazine

13.—AYLESBURY AND BUCKINGHAM.

Incorporated by 23 and 24 Vic , cap. 192 (6th Aug., 1860), to construct a line from the town of Aylesbury to join the Buckinghamshire at Claydon Junction. Length, 12¼ miles. Capital, 98,000*l.*, in 25*l.* shares; calls, 10*l.* per share, with intervals of two months. Loans, 32,500*l.* Extra land, two acres; compulsory purchase, two years; completion of works, five years. Working arrangements, under usual restrictions, with London and North Western and Buckinghamshire. Works in progress.

CAPITAL.—The statement of this account to 30th June composed the following particulars in relation to income and expenditure :—

Received.		*Expended.*	
Calls	£49,801	Parliamentary	£1,295
In anticipation of calls	1,210	Engineering	2,653
Loans on debentures	29,750	Land and compensation	2,200
		Works, &c.	54,102
		Advertising, &c.	116
		Law	1,312
		Aylesbury Joint Station	122
		Balance of interest account, &c.	2,794
		Office expenses	649
		Balance at bankers'	15,513
	£80,761		£80,761

No. of Directors—9; minimum, 3; quorum, 4; and 2 when reduced to 3. *Qualification,* 250*l.*

DIRECTORS :

Chairman—His Grace the DUKE of BUCKINGHAM and CHANDOS, Wotton, Aylesbury, and Stowe Park, Buckingham.

Deputy-Chairman— Sir HARRY VERNEY, Bart., M.P., Claydon House, Winslow, Bucks.

G. G. Pigott, Esq., Doddershall Park, Winslow, Bucks.
T. E. Foakes, Esq., 4, New Square, Lincoln's Inn, London, W.C.

John Lee, Esq., LL.D., Hartwell House Aylesbury.
J. K. Fowler, Esq., Aylesbury.

OFFICERS.—Sec., J. G. Rowe; Eng., W. M. Brydone, 5, Whitehall, Westminster, S.W.; Auditors, John Edward Bartlett, Aylesbury, and Henry Hearn, Buckingham; Solicitor, Thomas D. Calthrop, 8, Whitehall Place, Westminster, S.W.
Offices—5, Queen's Square, Westminster, S.W.

Composition of the Aylesbury & Buckingham Railway and its works in Bradshaw's Shareholders' Directory of 1864. Local railway promoters led the then Duke of Buckingham, as yet to be renegaded upon by the L&NWR who are mentioned in the working arrangements (note expenditure already mentioned for their joint station). The 'Buckinghamshire' is in fact the Buckinghamshire Railway at the other end of the line at Verney Junction, Chairman of this line being the same herementioned, Sir Harry Verney. Secretary of the Aylesbury & Buckingham Railway, Mr J. G. Rowe, managed the line when it was opened, together with the Watlington branch of the GWR. His name is raised many times in his managerial role on the A&BR in numerous clashes with his counterpart on the dependent line, the Wotton Tramway Manager, R. A. Jones. Local landed interests are further involved with G. G. Pigott Esq., of Doddershall Park which stands near the curve of the line at Quainton. The home of John Lee, Esq., Hartwell House, was also close to the line, just north of Aylesbury where it had its own siding. This was probably for coal. Later, several oil tanks were situated there. As this is included in a shareholders' guide, it is notable that the A&BR never achieved the distinction of paying its investors a dividend.

Rev. B. Edmunds

However, the struggling A&BR were soon to find that their alternative partner had not come to their rescue purely out of philanthropy, as the echo of old wars between the GWR and the L&NWR resolved into occasional competitive clashes, with one now at Aylesbury. The GWR tried its best to draw traffic from the latter's main and ancilliary lines, laying great emphasis on their London route via the Wycombe branch, whilst the A&BR survived as only a side-show, virtually hemmed in and ignored by both companies. Doubtless fate twisted against them once more when the General Manager of the GWR, James Grierson, offered to absorb the company. Preliminary negotiations were rather abruptly terminated with his death on 7th October 1887. His successor, unfortunately for the A&BR, was not of the same persuasion and dropped the matter altogether.

It would appear that this modest thread of line had been ill-starred from its inception in 1845. Although it had become a reality thirty years later, its prospects remained uncertain and its through running purpose did not find favour at either end of the line. However, its isolation did eventually prove to be something of an advantage in the 1890s' schemes of the advancing Metropolitan Railway, that had only begun to move northwards in the same year that the A&BR opened for business. Later, the A&BR would have an even greater prominence as part of a section of a grand trunk route to the north, with the opening of the Great Central Railway in 1899. By then, it would at last have achieved the ideal of its earliest inception.

The driving force behind these later schemes was embodied significantly in one man, Sir Edward Watkin, who was in fact no stranger to the region, as he once served as Secretary to the newly formed Buckinghamshire Railway. His Brunellian vision encompassed the idea of a trunk line running from the industrious North of England and Midlands thence to London, passing through the capital and on to the south-eastern corner, where it would link up with a new channel tunnel and complete a rail link on to the Continent. Although his efforts to convince the nascent Metropolitan Railway proved fruitless beyond the scheme of developing London suburbia north, he had rather more success with the north-country company, the Manchester, Sheffield & Lincolnshire Railway.

Events that led, first of all, to the Metropolitan Railway absorbing the entire A&BR and extending their influence to Verney Junction, closely followed by the lines being worked jointly by the Metropolitan & GCR, does, to a large degree, pre-empt the chronological flow of the course of this book and its central issue, which concerns the Wotton Tramway. This, therefore, leaves the first part of the story concerning the Aylesbury & Buckingham Railway at the point of its working arrangement with the GWR.

In one very distinct way, this can be regarded as a very tantalising glimpse of Verney Junction, for it is almost certainly taken during the period when the station was much more frugal and austere, before later developments and rebuilding would change it extensively. Ticket office, waiting-rooms and womens' lavatories were then part of the stationmaster's house; in fact, the only architectural structure, if one does not count the short empty platforms with only a tiny shelter and mens' urinal with sundry lamps. An aid to dating the period is the sign itself, which displays: 'Verney Junction — Change for Buckingham, Banbury and the Aylesbury and Buckingham Line'. A very similar, later, sign included the Metropolitan who, along with the L&NWR, had the station rebuilt. Although it would have been of tremendous interest to have had a photographic glimpse along those early platforms, doubtless the photographer felt that he held all that was worthwhile at this spot somewhat picturesquely within his frame. He is standing on the field side of the 'V' gates from the footpath level crossing at the end of the platform.

T. North

A photograph of very rare value is this view of the earliest connection of the Tramway at the first Quainton Road Station, which is clearly visible behind the train. Attention to diagrams would be a useful aid in examining this picture. The wagons are standing on the siding belonging to the Aylesbury & Buckingham Railway, and made available for the Tramway. Between them and the train is the road to Quainton village, on the other side of the hedge. The unsleepered, bridge rail, track is clearly visible. Further along the train is the turntable upon which is standing the GWR milk van, and behind that are two shallow wagons and, finally, the early passenger composite, with the guard standing on the nearest end to the camera. On the original print, a faint wooden semaphore is just visible behind the sheeted wagon on the siding. The white wooden fencing, between the engine and station building, surrounds the horse landing. Under magnification the words 'Quainton Road' are visible under the narrow overhanging roof of the station building, which appears to be just two rooms entered by doors at each end, obviously with two fireplaces. Details of the Tramway engine *Wotton* are as follows: cylinders 8in. x 12in., both inside between the two axles and driving on the leading axle. The boiler was placed high enough to give an even distribution of weight, with 4 tons 10 cwt. over the leading axle and 5 tons over the trailing axle. The total weight in working order 10 tons 5 cwt. The engine was designed to be fuelled on wood, and had a 200 gallon water tank placed between the boiler and the frame; a well tank, in fact and there was provision for 3 cwt. of coal. The boiler was 7ft. 3in. long and had a diameter of 2ft. 6in. Heating surface was 194 sq. ft. with a working steam pressure of 120p.s.i. It was capable of hauling 90 tons up a 1 in 100 incline, and 41 tons up a gradient of 1 in 44. The wheels of such endeavour were 2ft. 6in. in diameter on a base of 6ft. 3in., and each was distributed with a sandpipe, but did not have brakes. The overall length of the engine was 17ft. 2in.

Andrew Emmerson Collection

The Wotton Tramway

One of the excellent S. W. A. Newton photographs of the scene at Quainton Road a few years after the rebuilding of the station. Note the comparatively fresh mortar in the platform brick coursing on the right. The driver of engine *Brill No. 1*, Harry Cross, seen close to the spectacle plate, must have felt that he and his engine were celebrities, as he appears to have been an often photographed driver. On the footplate with him is Arthur Bayliss, whilst others are unknown station staff. The Midland Railway five plank wagons have probably returned from the branch after a coal delivery, with the brake third of the Oldbury stock in the rear.

S. W. A. Newton/Leicester County Council

During the early meeting at Wotton House, when the gentlemen wishing to promote the Aylesbury & Buckingham Railway met the then Chairman of the L&NWR, the Duke of Buckingham, they were greatly heartened by his support for their plans. His interest was stimulated by their acceptance of his suggested deviation of the line, four miles to the west of Pitchcott Gap, bringing it closer to the Duke's estates.

When the A&BR finally opened in 1868, his plans for an estate tramway could then go ahead, with a link with the new line at Quainton Road. The Tramway was first of all planned to run as far as the Duke's home at Wotton; a distance of 3¾ miles. This plan, however, was revised and he decided to extend the line, as near as it was cheaply possible to construct, to the village of Brill. The entire line was to be built on the Duke's estates, with the exception of a section at Quainton, which belonged to the Winwood Charity Trust, and a section at Westcott that had been newly-purchased by the Baron Ferdi-

nand de Rothschild. Providing he was able to conclude satisfactory arrangements with both parties, the Duke would not be required to put a Bill for building his line before Parliament, a good saving both in time and expense. Furthermore, as long as the line was protracted as a light agricultural railway, Board of Trade requirements made less rigorous demands. A horse-drawn speed limit of some four or five miles an hour over private land, and intended only for agriculture and livestock, was outside the spectrum of public concern, although five public road crossings did suggest marginal requirement for approval. The line was also covered by an Act of 14th August 1871 which allowed the Board of Trade to sanction railways of certain conditions; a maximum load of eight tons per axle, locomotive or vehicle, and a speed limit of 12m.p.h. In the event, the Duke was able to conclude agreement with all parties concerned.

Actual construction of the Tramway began on 8th September 1870, as labour became displaced from the surrounding farms

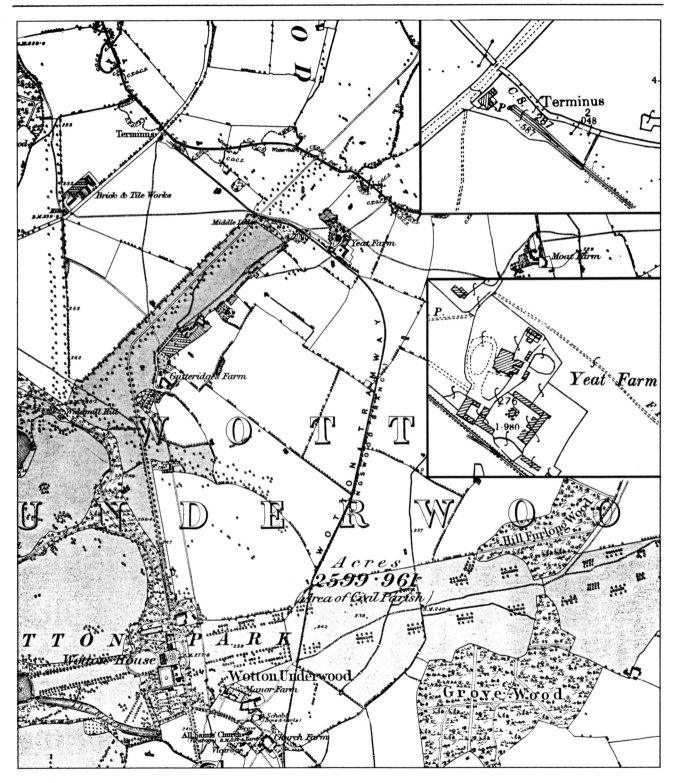

The route of the Kingswood branch, when still in use in 1883. All of this entire section was cut-back during World War I to the point at the bottom of the map, Church Siding. Passing in front of Wotton House it followed the edge of two large fields before sweeping across a third to pass almost through the farmyard of Yeat Farm (*see inset and stump of short siding*). From Yeat Farm, it made a reverse curve to take a parallel course leading it into its terminus on the Kingswood Lane (*see other inset*). Here a dwelling was built by the Duke for employees working at the coal wharf and the nearby Wotton Brick & Tile Works, which is visible further along the lane. Note the small rectangle of the end-loading ramp at the end of one of the terminal roads, useful for the loading of bricks and tiles.

Ordnance Survey

(Above): Engine No. 41 is seen about to pass over the first road crossing after Quainton Road Station with its single Metropolitan coach, circa 1930. The guard can be seen, shirtsleeved, just behind the signpost, as he prepares to close the gates after the train has passed over. It was from a pond, very close to this spot, that the Aveling Porter engines drew water in 1872.

R. W. Kidner

(Below): A scale drawing of one of the crossing gates at the first crossing (*as the above photograph*).

Mike Crosbie

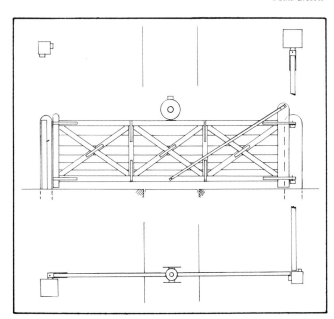

after the harvest. Twenty labourers were employed for six days a week at eleven shillings (55p) per week. The rather specialised task of laying the rails was carried out by the contractors, Lawford & Houghton, who laid the bridge pattern rail rolled by Townend & Wood of Briton Ferry, South Wales, which weighed 30lbs. a yard and cost £8 2s. 6d. (£8. 12½p) per ton, as delivered to Quainton Road. These were laid as a single line and fastened by flange bolts on to longitudinal timber baulks 6in. square and held rigid by transom sections tied at 12ft. intervals, holding for a standard gauge of 4ft. 8½ins. At the joints, a piece of oak acted as a fishplate through the hollow of the bridge pattern rail. Baulk construction allowed for the ease of horse hauling power, providing an unsleepered pathway of earth between the rails. Some ballast was composed of burnt clay, which had been dug on the estate, whilst ash was also used, brought from elsewhere. This was laid 15in. deep with 9in. of the larger bottom ballast.

Apart from the costly nature of earthworks, in view of the modest traction envisaged, it would be prudent to maintain the Tramway at as near level grades as possible, and this was largely achieved with some short, but severe, exceptions. The originally-planned terminus at Wotton was reached in March 1871, and this was 50ft. beneath the level of Quainton, which made the gradients favourable working from the main junction. The steepest section was at 1 in 54. Thereafter, as the line extended to Brill, it rose quite steeply on various climbs of 1 in 98, 1 in 50 and 1 in 64 on the curve of 9½ chains radius into the terminus; an overall ascent of 130ft. over 2½ miles — no line for laggered horses.

A striking view of the approaches to the first station at Waddesdon. From Quainton the railway and the road are divided by the hedge, an arrangement that ceased at this station, as the railway continues across into the fields. The hill to Waddesdon Manor rises up on the left. Just beyond the loading gauge is the single point lever that controls access to the siding.

L&GRP/Courtesy David & Charles

The dangers of railway construction were countlessly reiterated throughout the nineteenth century, and found emphasis even on this very minor enterprise when, on 31st December 1871, 'William Shepherd who, with others, was engaged in shunting a truck of materials used in the construction of the line at Brill, made a false step when he was struck by the brake which fractured his skull and inflicted injuries from which he is not expected to recover' pessimistically concluded the *Bucks Herald.*

The paper was able to speak warmly of some advantage offered by the building of the line in its columns, when it spoke of employment which it had provided during the severe winter season, noting also with special praise for the Duke, who had distributed coal free from the first train to bring it to Wotton, amongst the poor of the parish. For it was on 1st April 1871, that the Duke was able to perform a little ceremony recognising the opening of the line from Quainton to Wotton, which would allow this part to be brought into use whilst the next section from Wotton to Brill could be worked upon. Thame Lodge was reached by June 1871. Wood Siding, where the 7,000 year old fragment of the ancient Bernwood Forest, called Rushbeds Wood, first echoed to the sound of iron hammering and flanged wheels rolling on 19th August 1871. Although the little station to be situated at this spot would become remarkable for its silvan isolation and pictorialise a summer ideal, it was anything but a summer prospect in the

remarks of Ralph Augustus Jones, who would superintend the construction of the line, and manage its limitations with great patience and skill in the coming years. He communicated to the Duke of the heavy going in the extensive rain, in the season which made progress and running very dangerous for the horses. They slipped so badly in the waterlogged clay, that burnt ballast was piled on to give the horses some sure footing and soak the cloying mud.

Cottons Lane Gate was the next notable point in the line's construction and this was reached on 29th November, whereupon a siding was put in for the use of several brickworks operating in and around the village of Brill. The actual siding into the Brill Brickworks that arrived on this site circa 1895, was not put in across the road until shortly after this date. Up until that time, the siding, as mentioned in construction, was arranged parallel with the road.

From this point to the site of Brill Station, the line encountered its only cutting, not made any easier by the gradient on a sharp curve, before finally rolling into the station site in March 1872. It had cost £1,400 per mile to construct including sidings, cattle landings, stables and two commodious goods sheds. As explained, this figure does not include any cost for land, being within the estate.

The people of Brill were gratified that the Duke had extended his Tramway to serve their needs, but felt that it should also

The long view from Waddesdon Road Station, looking in the Quainton direction. Alongside the road is the one time very familiar road junction warning sign, beneath a triangle set in a circle. The road junction is behind the camera. Note Waddesdon goods shed alongside the offices on the right.

London Transport Executive

include the facility of a passenger service. In fact, this requirement had been pressed upon him before Brill was actually reached when the construction was still in the vicinity of Wood Siding. For, on 21st August 1871, 150 redoubtable excursionists, including an appreciable proportion of local schoolchildren, enthusiastically entrained on a special train to London. People from Westcott, Wotton and Ashendon joined at various points after leaving Wood Siding at 5.30a.m. In all probability, this first account of a passenger train on the line consisted of GWR stock, for at Aylesbury it was attached to the normal 7.30a.m. service train to London, which finally brought the villagers into the capital at 10a.m. The motive power between Wood Siding and Aylesbury must, however, remain a fascinating mystery on which to ponder. The return of the excursionists was not quite so expiditiously concluded, as a long delay was incurred at Slough to allow the 'mails' to pass. The final arrival back to the dark woodland recess of their original station was not accomplished until well past midnight, which must have concluded a memorable but lengthy day.

The Duke must have drawn a great deal of satisfaction from the opening of the full length of the Tramway, which was earning £50 per week, for it was only some twelve months later

that he embarked his labour force on building another twig from the main branch, with another set of rails from a point near to Wotton Station to a point near the estate's brick and tile works on Kingswood Lane *(see map)*. This branch from a branch was of the same light construction and extended for 1 mile and 57 chains. A coal wharf was installed at the end, and the facility of a turntable was constructed. A siding was arranged alongside and there was also a dwelling for a member of the Duke's staff. Approximately midway along this branch, a serviceable pond was made use of to slake the thirst of the horses hauling the trucks, which was the basic method of refreshing the animal haulage on the entire Tramway; even after the arrival of the first steam locomotives to be used on the line. However, it was not a reliable or desirable method of replenishing the tubular innards of machines, and a water-tower was built in the 'V' of this branch line junction which was known as Springfield watertower, or locally, as the 'black tank'. Wotton was, in fact, the important point on the line, not only because of the junction nearby but also for the large stables where all the horses were kept to work the system. Connection with the Aylesbury & Buckingham line at Quainton was by the means of a 13ft. turntable which must have caused a laborious bottleneck to the

Waddesdon Road Station, as seen from the road junction of the lane leading down to Quainton on the left, and the direct route, Akeman Street, leading on to Aylesbury. Note the overlapped crossing gates.

London Transport Executive

service of trucks moving on to and off the Tramway. The turntable was installed in December 1870, and was bought for £99 14s. 0d. (£99.70) from Bridgewater Ironworks.

The installation of this was due to the right angle position of the Tramway to the main line alongside. There was also a siding put in for use of the Tramway. Although any goods carried up to March 1871 are confused with the tonnages required for the construction of the line, the metals did in fact carry 3,200 tons which, at 6½ tons per wagon, would require quite a few revolutions of that turntable! A proper junction with the A&BR was eventually formed in 1893. This was elaborated further with the resiting of the Quainton Road Station by the Metropolitan Railway who took over the running of the A&BR in 1891.

Buildings along the Tramway were practically all of timber construction, with the exception of the dwellings for the staff which were built in brick, in the style of other estate cottages. There were no buildings at all belonging to the Tramway at Quainton, nor were there any at the site of the second station at Waddesdon where the Tramway crossed the Bicester to Aylesbury Road (the Roman Akeman Street). A siding was put in at this point by the Tramway; doubtless a farm and coal siding. Competitively, the village of Waddesdon did not receive another station until the opening of the Waddesdon Manor Station on the A&BR on 1st January 1897.

At Westcott, the 'platform' of piled sods was adjoining two substantial cottages for the occupation of Tramway staff. At this station a siding was also put in for the same use. Of particular interest in this area are the developments concerning the building of Waddesdon Manor, the home of the Baron Ferdinand de Rothschild. After purchase of 2,700 acres, including Lodge Hill, work began in 1876 with levelling off the top of the hill, and lasted for fifteen years until the splendid array of French style turrets and gables began to rise out of the amorphous confusion of construction. An important aid to this extensive work was a branch laid in from the Tramway between Waddesdon and Westcott stations, in standard gauge. This extended from the line as far up the hill as normal adhesion haulage would tolerate. Locomotives did not work this siding (it was operated by horses) as an attempt to use a locomotive soon ended in derailment, which left the entire burden at the resource of the familiar working horse. Their rote of hill climbing and descending was mundane, by comparison with another heavy horse occupation here. This was the resiting of mature trees around the newly-constructed Manor. Large teams of mighty Percheron mares, imported from Normandy, hauled the chained girths of Lime, Elm and Chestnut from all parts of the neighourhood to the site of this incredible replanting operation. Percheron mares were used for this as they were faster and cheaper than English Shire horses.

Returning to the subject of the contractor's siding from the Tramway, at the point where equine power ceased, there was a narrow gauge railway to carry the materials in smaller trucks or tubs the rest of the way uphill; this was operated by cable haulage with a steam winch. At the junction of the gauges, a run-round loop was installed.

To give some indication of the busy use of this siding and the Tramway that served it are the following details. Bricks came from both the Quainton and Brill directions. Poore's brick-works at Brill supplied 25,000 bricks per week, whilst 7,000 tons of Batch stone came from Corsham in Wiltshire, via Verney Junction, along with 700 tons of roadstone for foundations. This was all in the first year. Needless to say there would be considerable consignments of timber, with no small amount being supplied from the Duke's estate at Wotton.

There was a temporary halt to construction for three years from 1880, but the Manor was finally completed in 1889. As a signature of the highest recognition, Her Majesty Queen Victoria made an official visit there on 14th May 1890. The honour of her conveyance was not unfortunately accorded the A&BR, for she travelled on the GWR from Windsor to Aylesbury and then by horse-drawn carriage from the station to the Manor.

Perceptively viewing the Manor's steady progress and completion, R. A. Jones looked to the day when the traffic it brought to the line would cease, and tried to interest the Duke in the opening of a brickworks of more extensive manufacture near Brill; this was in 1885. He estimated that it would cost £3,000 to build and, from the excellent quality of the brickmaking clay, could produce five million bricks a year. The Duke must have viewed the suggestion with some interest, as a new concept of that industry was introduced to the Brill district as a result. By 1895, the Brill Brick & Tile Company was in business manufacturing bricks by the new mass production 'Fletton' process, which must have caused a competitive jolt to the slower hand-making works in the area. R. A. Jones became Managing Director of the works, which employed up to one hundred men. Again, the Tramway was able to provide a siding by extending an existing farm siding across the road and running right into the works, which is essential with the 'Fletton' process. Access to waiting demand would be found beyond the Tramway through Quainton Road and later with the building of the Great Central Railway.

From the outset, Waddesdon Manor was able to take advantage of the development of coal gas which instigated thousands of tiny plants all over the country. The Manor started to build its own works, on the outskirts of the village of Westcott, in a field next to Westcottfield Farm. This was opened at the same time as the Manor, 1889. The coal supply was brought via Quainton Road Station and along the Tramway, where a siding leading to the works was put in alongside the Westcott to Ashendon Road, passing through the gates of a field where the gasworks was situated.

In the gasworks structure, there were retorts in which the coal was roasted to produce coke and coal gas. Coal gas, a mixture of hydrogen, carbon monoxide and methane, had a number of impurities, ammonia, tar, sulphur compounds and water vapour. The impure gas was passed through water filters to remove the tar and ammonia, then through layers of lime to remove the sulphur. Finally it was fed into the single one-lift gasholder with a diameter of 40ft. and approximately 12ft. high.

Gas from the works was piped to the Manor, its laundry and stables, whilst the by-products of tar and ammonia were taken from the site by rail to Quainton and on to Silvertown Works in London.

The operation of the works was very much a local affair; the Manager, Mr Albert Evans, had learned the art of gas making from his father Mr J. Evans, who administered that function at Mr Lionel de Rothschild's house at Ascott, near Wing. From there, he came to administer the Waddesdon Estates, in 1883. He continued successfully to perform this duty throughout the life of the works, which was curtailed by the scarcity of coal supplies during World War I. This brought about its closure, in 1916, when its purpose had been supplanted by an electric generator, also on the estate.

The next station along the line was Wotton, near the 4¼ mile post and closest to Wotton House and the line's junction. This gave Wotton special significance. Here was built one of the two timber goods sheds on the line, this one measuring 21ft. x 30ft., whilst the capacious installation at Brill measured 60ft. x 25ft. More special to Wotton was the construction of the stables, originally rectangular, and this timber structure probably enclosed a forge and farrier facilities, in view of it being a central point for the distribution of horse power on the lines. Other features of the Wotton installation were the cattle pen facilities and an end-loading ramp for carts, coaches and various horse-drawn vehicles. Like Westcott, a matching pair of estate cottages were built to house Tramway staff.

From Wotton, the line curved away past All Saints Church of Wotton Underwood and across open fields until crossing the driveway to Wotton House, alongside the lodge known as Thame Lodge, nearby, on the 4¾ milepost point. Another short siding was put in here to serve the estate and probably the estate blacksmith, who lived near Thame Lodge, who had his forge close by. His name was Charles Roberts and, undoubtedly, he would be called upon many times to make, repair and maintain vehicles and parts of the Tramway, but his most fitting memorial must be the splendid wrought-iron gates that still adorn the front of Wotton House to this day and are credited to him.

Curving once more, the line reached the vicinity of Rushbeds Woods, a portion of that more ancient source, the Bernwood Forest. Alongside the crossing gates, where the line passed over the Dorton to Ludgershall road, was the very minor outpost of Wood Siding Station, the originating point of the early reference to a London excursion, although the comparison with London as a destination from Wood Siding is remote in the extreme. Interestingly, this spot was manned by a relative of Charles Roberts, the blacksmith, Alfred Roberts, who looked after the crossing gates and loaded and unloaded merchandise, on the single siding; very often this was milk. It is understood that the small corrugated hut that appeared at this spot in later years was not in situ originally, which would have made this locality an occupation of some privation had not the dwelling where Alfred Roberts lived not been close by, a matter of a few hundred yards along the Ludgershall Road where there is an interesting group of cottages. Unlike the estate style cottages apparent at other stations on the line, these rejoice in the heroic name of 'Waterloo Cottages'. A memorial to a

Jimmy Reeves with his dog at Westcott Station during the 1930s.

John Pritchett Collection

A crude but original diagram of the earliest connection of the Tramway with the Aylesbury & Buckingham Railway. The small station of one short platform and a single station building included a horse landing and a siding. Wotton Tramway is connected to the main line via this siding, and has a loop that was installed in May 1876. The connecting line then crosses the road, intersecting the Tramway proper across the small turntable. It is obviously not an arrangement to suit volume traffic and, understandably, did prove contentious between the railways. Sometime during the 1880s, a more sensible arrangement was met, with a proper connection being put in with direct running on and off the A&BR, no doubt in prospect that one day the line would eventually reach Oxford. However, it was the burgeoning development of the Metropolitan Railway that rebuilt the A&BR, and put an end to the entire arrangement at this spot with the resiting of Quinton Road Station.

Mike Crosbie

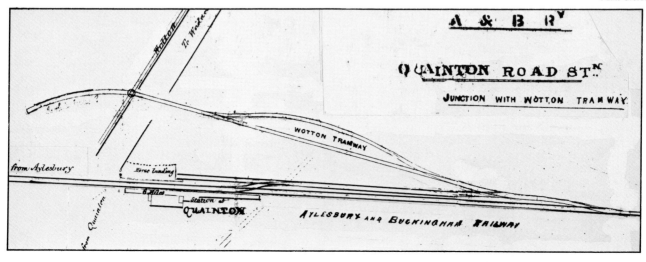

There is a secret foliant lushness about Wotton Station that remains at the site to this day. In the changeless demesne of the environs of Wotton House, the line threads a landscape inured with centuries of harvesting and pasture, with a hardy resistance to the twentieth century. When Newton took this photograph, during the construction of the GW&GC Joint line, which is unseen behind the trees, he froze into illustration a remarkable period. A glance at the early diagram of the station, in Wotton Tramway times, will show that the platform did not exist, originally, nor the hut-office, waiting-rooms, lavatories, etc., but the goods shed did. As drawings of this are included in this publication, it is possible to build a miniature representation of one of the very few early Tramway structures. Unfortunately, not every building is clearly understood; one mystery is the stables, beyond the wagons in the siding. Diagrams show this as a rectangular building, and there is only this photograph to support that, albeit evident only by a view of the roof. In respect of the importance of this building's function, especially in early Tramway days, with horses being supplied from here for all the system, it seems reasonable that part of the building would be a smith and farrier installation. A small plume of smoke in the centre of the roof-line lends support to this view. Further enlightenment is not to hand and, as photographs and drawings in this publication will show, the building was greatly shortened before 1935. The siding visible in this view is the same that was extended over the trackbed of the 'Joint' during construction.

S. W. A. Newton/Leicester County Council

One of the short wooden staffs used to control train occupation on the line. Although very faint, it is still possible to see on the original photograph the names, 'Brill — Wotton' on each side of circular scoring. Train staffs along the line were issued thus: Quainton — Wotton (Blue), Wotton — Brill (Red), Kingswood branch (Red).

Buckinghamshire County Museum

confrontation of the kind that would not be unknown to Alfred, who was a veteran of 25 years army service.

Further along the line, up to the 5½ milepost, was another of the many sidings that ran off the system. At first, this siding was quite short and arranged alongside the Brill to Dorton road. Normal use for such short sidings tended to be as catchment points for loading and unloading agricultural produce or coal. This particular siding had an extra use, serving the small brick and tile industry that flourished in the village of Brill. Later a large factory for this business was built, circa 1890, facing the siding, where a farm had been. The siding was then given an additional storage loop and extended across the road into this new factory, so that wagons could be shunted into a trench on a loading level, which would allow bricks to be wheeled in from the stacking shed into the open wagon, minimising handling.

The Brill Brick & Tile Company prospered when large scale manufacture was in its infancy and demand was very high. This was between the earlier time of the slow hand-making process, using plastic top callow, fired in small kilns and serving parochial outlets, but before the massive scale manufacture of the large plants and deep pits of the London Brick Company. Even this Brill works was to feel the shock wave of this latter concern especially when a plant was opened at the turn of the century at Calvert, some seven or eight miles away. The output of the Calvert plant was modestly termed in millions per week rather than thousands. By 1905, it was competition that the Brill works could not withstand and it closed in that year.

Continuing along the remainder of the final short distance to Brill Station would mean climbing a 1 in 64 gradient on 9½ chain radius curves, through the line's only cutting. The station of Brill would become visible almost on a slight peak, laid in the angle of a field which dropped away quite sharply.

Somewhat beyond the age of popular photography, the Brill Station of the Wotton Tramway period can only be imagined from diagrams, and from what remains on more contemporary illustrations. Even the earliest diagram of 1883 is believed to have been slightly modified from the original terminus. One of the earliest buildings is the large train shed, which served collectively as a goods shed, passenger station and booking office. There is also a small hut, with a set of rails going into it. This probably housed the first steam locomotive. Water supply was advantaged from a well nearby, around which was built a circular brick top. Presumably another building was used as stables. At first, two cottges existed alongside the station for the housing of Tramway employees; as a small holidng this came to be known as Tramway Farm. A third cottage was added to this group in 1885, presumably for extra staff, as the Tramway was at that time in prospect of further development. There was also a brick and timber blacksmith's forge at the station. Precise dates of two small store buildings is difficult to pin-point as these could have been built fairly quickly at any time. What is known is that they held the local supply of ale brought up the line to slake the thirst of some of the numerous pubs in Brill village. One of the stores is known to have been the storage building for the brewery of Hopcroft & Norris of Brackley. Later their interests in the building were taken over by the Aylesbury Brewery Company (ABC).

That concludes a description of the appearance of the Tramway as it existed for the first twenty years of its life; lightly-constructed with few buildings, a dozen or so short sidings and platforms built of earth. In a country that has passed through the heat of a railway boom with engineering marvels seemingly thrown up almost overnight, the little Tramway would not draw more than local interest. It was merely a microcosm of the railway age, occasionally revealing itself from the trees to disrupt the progress of some road traveller at a crossing, or to be seen making its snail's pace across the arable field to disappear beyond the hedgerow.

Administration of its business had been, from the outset, very much in the hands of the Duke's appointed Manager, Ralph Augustus Jones. A local man who also managed the brickworks at Brill, he helped with the survey for the line and became inextricably linked with it. His anxious report to the Duke of the sodden earthworks between Thame Lodge and Wood Siding during construction presaged innumerable worries for three decades afterwards, as he tried to maintain the service of the line against its inherent shortcomings, and from a very thin purse. Doubtless, Jones was aware of the advantages of railways, not only for agriculture but for the tremendous difference they made to brick and tile production, both in heavy demand at that time, as drain tiles for land had found great favour.

He was employed on the line through the Duke's agents Chaplin & Horne, who had themselves formed an integral part of Britain's transportation revolution.

During the coaching years, William Chaplin had owned more than 3,000 road coaches and wagons, 150,000 horses and, by 1836, two years before the opening of the London & Birmingham Railway, employed 30,000 drivers, guards and ostlers. Each night, the company despatched 27 mail coaches out of London. With the development of the railways he adroitly steered the firm to serving rail connection, especially for the London & Birmingham Railway and its successor the London & North Western Railway. The interests of the company survive to the present day, in the form of that famous carrier group, Pickfords.

As already mentioned, stations of the Wotton Tramway were makeshift affairs as impromptu as the trains that called at them; they were, themselves, a mixed assembly. Anything was put with anything, and whilst the rest of Britain developed traffic systems that dealt with passengers and goods in parallel but distinctly separate undertakings, hugely co-ordinated, the Brill branch never felt called upon to make the same distinction. The paucity of its traffic tends to make this self evident throughout its history.

Although a staff system was introduced, even the Tramway had to observe this rudimentary concession to safety; there was no signalling of special note except for that subsequently explained. Since the line was intended to work on the one engine in steam principle, or two coupled together, this would prove acceptable. However, early traction was not concerned with steam, save that risen by the flanks of horses, but even on this light line this motive power could not be endured indefinitely.

The ever resourceful horse plied its way with the early Tramway service of both goods and passengers, each unloaded wagon weighing 3½ tons and capable of holding 6 to 7 tons. Two horses would be allotted to three wagons, except when encountering the steeper gradients near Brill, where two horses would take only one wagon at a time. Although wagons of ten tons gross were sometimes used on the line, it was a wary fact that ten tons per axle was the absolute maximum for such lightly-built track, not to mention overworking the horses. The equestrian motive power although dependable to a fault, was to prove, as railways discovered before, a moribund restriction to developing traffic. The burgeoning steam locomotive would not be denied for

Aveling Porter engine No. 2, fitted with 4ft. 6in. wheels, in May 1881. They were put on to encourage greater stability, which was a serious problem when these engines were under load. Little, if anything, appears to be known of the consequences of shortening the chimney. In this view of the drive side of the engine transmission, the horizontal cylinder is clearly seen, with piston rod to shaft and flywheel. The heavy chain encircling the toothed drive shaft and both axles is also clearly evident. It is believed that the gentleman in the tall hat on the right is the Duke of Buckingham and Chandos.

London Transport Executive

There is little photographic evidence of the period of the Wotton Tramway, but this print is amongst the few. It is of Aveling Porter engine No. .1, somewhere on the line, which is still bridge rail on timber baulks. The understandable precaution of a spark arrestor has been added to the engine's chimney, whilst some weather protection is afforded for the crew by cab sheeting. The absurdly small spectacle plates give this engine a slightly humorous appearance, although this amount of cover was probably welcomed by the men confined on such tortuously slow journeys. Another addition to the engine since delivered, was a second buffer beam and draw gear fixed to the front. This was added in 1874 at the express wish of Jones, who complained of the added difficulties in having to make sure that the engine was smokebox first. The train comprises, first of all, a solid Great Western Railway brake van, followed by two ageing L&NWR cattle vans, and the end is completed by the shaky Tramway composite coach. This vehicle also required further attention when it was returned to the makers after only a year's service. It appears that, as a result of the rigid suspension, the end balconies became bent on the solebars.

London Transport Executive

(Above):   A view photographed sixty years later, at Nether Heyford Brickworks, in 1938, where No. 1 is still at work and looking more like her original condition, without cab and spark arrestor. As explained more fully in the text, her working days on the Tramway ended with the new proprietors of the Oxford & Aylesbury Tramway in 1894. From that time until 1940, both engines remained at the brickyard, although only one was used, as the other provided spares. After that date, No. 807 lay rusting in weedy dereliction in full view of the London to Birmingham main line, and may have passed into oblivion but for the good offices of the Industrial Locomotive Society who, in 1950, approached London Transport on the possibility of restoring the old Wotton engine. Fortunately, this they agreed to do, and have earned the immense gratitude of all railway interests, as it is now on public view amidst the splendour of the London Transport Museum at Covent Garden.

Mike Crosbie

(Below):   Springfield Water-Tower, or, as known by the staff and locals, the 'black tank', which was situated in the 'V' of the main line and branch line junction to Kingswood.

Mike Crosbie

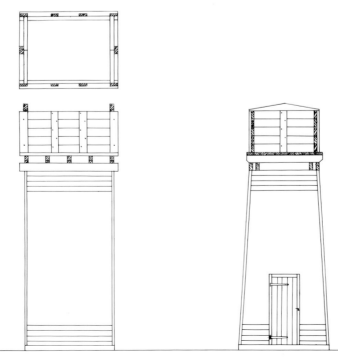

(Above): Where lines divide, at the 'black tank' as seen on 27th August 1932. The cast-iron plate notice alongside the field gate, on the right, is authorised by the 'Met. & GCR Joint Committee'. A fine detail in the distance is the point lever for the junction switch. *F. M. Gates/Lens of Sutton*

(Below): A plan diagram of the junction. *Mike Crosbie*

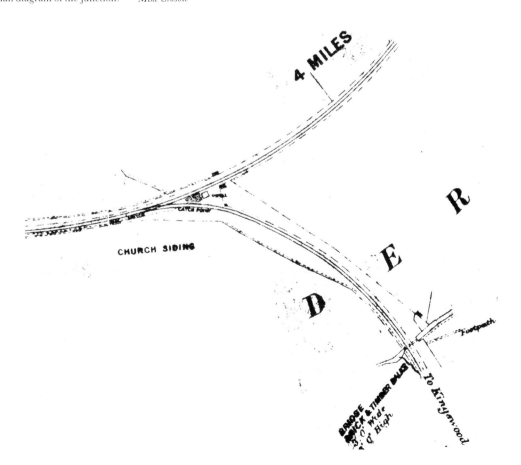

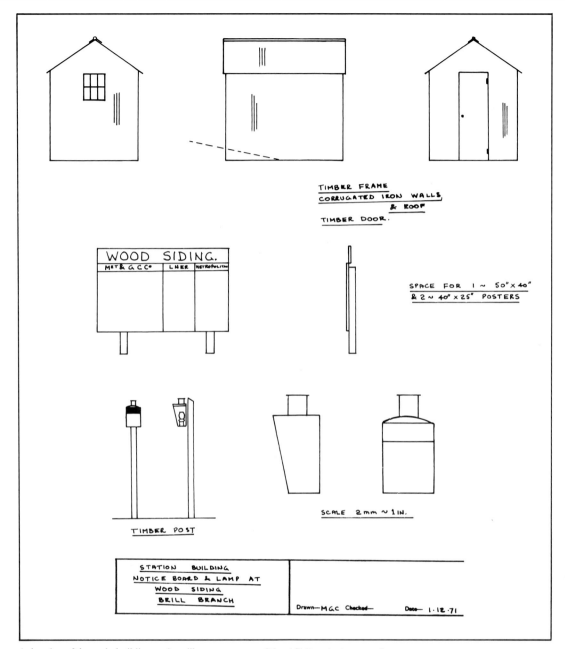

A drawing of the main building and ancillary structures at Wood Siding, in 4mm. scale.

Mike Crosbie

long. On 20th October 1871, Jones wrote to the Duke: 'The traffic is now becoming so heavy that I would most respectfully venture to ask your grace to consider the subject as to whether an engine would not be the least expensive and most efficient power to work it. At least as far as Westcott'. This erudite suggestion was not as simple as purchasing a steam locomotive and placing it on the track, even though the line was built to standard gauge, for the weight restriction of the spaced long baulk track design was expressly to provide a clear pathway for the horses, whilst a locomotive would be required to fall within the limited axle loading. No conventional machine at that time came close to this requirement.

However, a solution was found by the company of Aveling & Porter of Rochester in Kent; a locomotive that was the precursor of their famous steam road rollers. It was mounted on four flanged wheels, and tractive effort was drawn from a single cylinder, 7¾in. in diameter with a 10in. stroke mounted over the boiler and enclosed within a steam jacket. Drive was transmitted from a crankshaft and flywheel (3ft. 6in. dia.) on to spur gearing to a chain pinion. The shaft had slotted support brackets to raise and tension a chain drive around two wheels of one side of the engine. A pump connected to an eccentric on the drive shaft maintained a steady water supply from tanks both at the front and the back of the engine. Although a speed of

Wood Siding, seen from the roadway and looking down Kingswood Lane, where Alfred Roberts' home of Waterloo Cottages can be seen. The bridge carrying the railway over the Ashendon Junction to Aynho Junction line of the GWR can be seen on the left. One could easily imagine a mixed train being drawn very slowly across the scene by the Aveling Porter or Bagnall locomotive, or a horse, or the slightly greater haste of the Manning Wardle engine with its special Tramway coaches, before the sanguine red of the Metropolitan could contrast against the deep green of the huge oak tree that has witnessed it all. Note the piece of flat bottom rail, being used as a signpost, at the entrance to the siding yard in the centre of the picture. This rail may, like the bridge rail, have ceased its load-bearing activity many years previously but much of it never left the area, for it is often found to this day holding up fences and walls, retaining hedging and, in one example, assembled into a makeshift bridge for the farmer to cross a small stream!

London Transport Executive

5m.p.h. and drawbar of six horsepower would be useless to a railway of conventional demands, it did at least fall within the parameters of the weight restriction. This restriction would be a factor that would dog the railway until the trackbed was rebuilt with new rail, which was installed some twenty five years later.

Eventually, the Tramway purchased two of these engines, and the first was unloaded at Wotton Station, presumably drawn by horse and wagon from Quainton, on 27th January 1872. It was a welcome of greater zeal than contemplation, for the problem of unloading a driver at the same time had been overlooked. Thereby, in wonderous immobility, the new acquisition must stand until one could be found, whilst the horse traction continued to pass it aloofly by. Embarrassment did not remain at that, for some of the Tramway's beasts had been, as it seems, prematurely sold out of stock, and it must have been a little red-faced to hire them back.

However, *Tramway No. 1* (Works No. 807) did, at last, take up her duties in due course and 'old chainey's' rattle became a familiar sound between Quainton and Brill. Speed is not a

description that could very easily be applied to her progress, but an ability to haul 37 tons up a 1 in 50 gradient at 4m.p.h., and the same load at 8m.p.h. on the level, was considered a distinct improvement. Sufficiently it appeared to warrant another £398 being spent on a sister engine as the existing engine had a limiting factor of being available to work only part of the day before the daily routine of fire dropping and ashpan cleaning needed to be undertaken. Into the high summer of June, the second engine arrived, *Tramway No. 2* (Works No. 846), to take up her duties alongside. The only drivers' view comment, that has filtered through by word of mouth over the years, is that the engine performed noticeably better when being worked chimney first. Although the sounds of steam were now echoing along the rails, it was still expedient to work the longer sidings of Gasworks and the Kingswood branch, by horse power.

With the introduction of steam power, the Tramway was earning £50 per week by December 1872, and Jones found it easier to introduce a better regular train working system. Not long after the driver had been put to work on the first

The Duke of Buckingham and Chandos.

National Portrait Gallery

passenger carrying railway, but could remain as a light goods tramway with traction engines running at low speed. Criticisms amounted to the following: track construction was too light, bridge rail 21ft. long — 30lbs. lineal yard, passenger platforms were inadequate (piled sods), and no shelter; there were no signals and interlocking, twelve sidings and no facing point locks. There were a number of sharp gradients, although quite short, 1 in 44 being the steepest. Comparable sharp curves abounded; 6½ chains at Quainton Road.

Most of the traction had been handled by horses after the opening in February 1871. Since then, a traction engine of 9 tons had been purchased. This could do a maximum speed of 7m.p.h., and could be brought to a standstill in 30 yards. On arrival at crossing gates the fireman jumped off the engine and with a red flag he stopped any road traffic before opening the gates. A passenger service had been operating and had a maximum number of people in August 1872 (456), but the average per train was about 6 to 8. In the same year, 3,200 tons of manure was carried which was dropped off at sidings or, as requested, in fields alongside the line.

The Board of Trade report on Colonel Yolland's findings was published in July 1873. A valuable addition to the slender knowledge of the early condition of the Tramway. A placative measure to the fact that the Duke had thus far proceeded largely without official certification, was his reference to the published Book of Rules under which the Tramway was earnestly operated.

Fares were 1s. 0d. (5p) from Brill, 6d. (2½p) from Wotton and 3d. (1p) from Westcott; the guard would issue tickets for those en route from his book whilst on the train.

Goods stock consisted of coal, bricks and tiles, hay, milk, casks of ale, manure and every imaginable commodity of farm merchandise including, of course, livestock. These were carried at a standard goods rate of 4d. (1½p) per cwt. The fleet of vehicles used to transport this merchandise consisted of nine four wheel wagons, some with 9in. sides and others with 11in. sides, and all dumb-buffered. These did not comply with Railway Clearing House regulations. There was also one four-wheeled

engine, Jones corresponded enthusiastically with the Duke on 6th February 1872 when he remarked that he brought the four coal trucks and the passenger van from Quainton to Wotton in 41 minutes on a Saturday night. The load represented 42 tons and with so many loads waiting at Quainton, he was going to work the engine through that afternoon, trying her with six loads of coal etc!

Early in 1873, the Duke made an attempt to have the line recognised as a proper railway. To implement this request the Board of Trade commissioned Inspector Colonel Yolland to report on the line on 2nd May 1873. The subsequent report did not recommend that the line could be sanctioned as a proper

Wotton Tramway Timetable — April 1873

	Down	1	2	3	4	5
leave	Brill	6.50			2.50	
	Wood Siding	7.00	On Sats.		3.00	
	Church Siding	7.10	only		3.10	
arrive	Wotton	7.13			3.13	
leave	Wotton	7.18	8.05	1.30	3.18	3.10
arrive	Westcott	7.43	8.25	1.50	3.38	3.30
arrive	Wadds. Rd.	7.49	8.33	1.58	3.51	3.42
arrive	Quainton	8.00	8.55	2.10	4.02	4.02
	Up	1	2	3	4	5
leave	Quainton	9.20	9.05	4.40	5.45	5.45
	Wadds. Rd.	9.33	9.20	4.53	5.58	6.00
	Westcott	9.39	9.30	4.59	6.04	6.10
arrive	Wotton	9.59	9.50	5.20	6.24	6.30
leave	Wotton	10.11			6.26	
arrive	Church Siding	10.06	On Sats.		6.29	
arrive	Wood Siding	10.21	only		6.45	
arrive	Brill	10.40			7.00	

No. 5 Trains will only run on Thursdays when No. 4 trains are not run
No. 5 Trains 'up' run on Saturdays
No. 3 Trains run to Wotton on Saturdays — instead of No. 4 and wait
there the arrival of No. 5 from Quainton

A view photographed around the same time at the Brill end of the station, almost on the spot that some ten years later was replaced by a plate girder bridge with the construction of the new GWR railway from Ashendon to Aynho. It is quite probable that the building of this line would bring about the rebuilding of Wood Siding platform at the height familiar on later photographs. There does not appear to be a loading gauge at Wood Siding at this time.

J. C. Barnes

Wood Siding, in Oxford & Aylesbury Tramroad days, around the 1898 period. There is little representation of the company by display; the only sign may well be a timetable nailed to the almost changeless oak. Obviously, the platform arrangement does suggest a certain order, with planks held in position with pieces of defunct bridge rail. Note the standard iron post and rail fencing.

J. C. Barnes

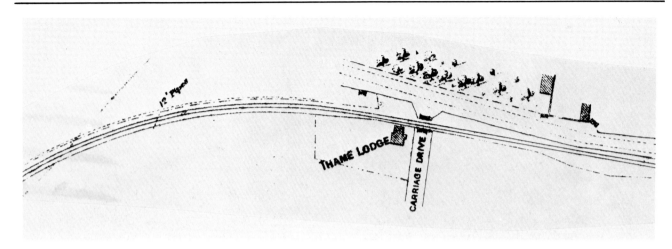

Thame Lodge, 1900. The only difference evident from earlier days is the removal of a short siding trailing in the 'up' direction, between the road and the rails. The lodge house is, of course, to administer access into the estate. Crossing gates would not require a keeper as the exception here was for the gates to be left open for the railway. A regulation speed limit of 4m.p.h. over the crossing, after an engine whistle, was to enforce greater vigilance by all parties.

Mike Crosbie

Thame Lodge, seen from the front of a train arriving from Quainton.

London Transport Executive

Brill Station, after a span of many years, on 6th October 1935. Nevertheless, a link with the beginning of the line is still retained in the presence of the large timber goods shed behind the station buildings. This was originally the entire station of Brill, acting as train shed, booking office and goods shed, and terminus of the Wotton Tramway. The coach is the last vehicle to be used on the line, a first/third composite of the Metropolitan Railway.

S. W. Baker

luggage van. All through traffic was handled in wagons or cattle trucks hired from either the GWR or L&NWR.

Subsequently, Jones was to discover the limits of his engines. As in all matters concerning expansion or development, the limits are inevitably found and these became manifest in this case by the engines lifting their front and dropping their wheels off the track on being consigned excessive haulages. A very halting limitation on progress. There were also further difficulties with tortuously slow journeys, often abbreviated by lack of steam power, chain breakages and derailments, not to mention some indifferent driving capabilities and neglected maintenance, which brought about more than one dismissal.

The light tramway track also suffered from being spread by the locomotives, and received no better attention. In short, the railway was quickly gaining a reputation for being unreliable, although, to be fair, it was suffering also from heavy usage. Unfortunately there was a litany of mishaps from November 1872 until October of the following year, an entire train of wagons coming off the line at Thame Lodge due to bad ballasting. A driving chain breakage caused not only the train's passengers to miss their connection at Quainton, but failed to deliver an entire milk supply. The slightly humorous complaint of the funnel breaking off at Quainton, must bear grim comparison to the flywheel suddenly coming off the engine in motion at Wood Siding and careering down the line for 12 to 15 yards, passing over a spot only shortly vacated by a fortunate flagman who would almost certainly have been killed. On a working mileage of only 130 a week, working progress was not good.

Chaplin & Horne estimated running expenses for the first year at £650, which included 10 per cent interest on the two engines; earnings were about £1,350. As already mentioned, in 1874 the construction of Waddesdon Manor began, and the demands on the Tramway, with its moribund haulage capabilities due to its light construction, was being tested even further. A review of the situation was put in hand which brought an arrangement with the other famous steam locomotive builder, W. G. Bagnall. As a result a miniscule, but more conventional, type of locomotive was hired from them and put into service on 1st January 1877.

To some degree, the Stafford company of W. G. Bagnall were interested in the results of their new design of light engine in service and offered this facility to the Wotton Tramway. It was an offer that must have found agreement with the often worried Jones, who was delighted to witness its hauling capabilities of 60 tons from Quainton to Brill, and 30 tons by return. On the little 'long drag' from Wotton to Brill, the terrier-like resolve of this little engine would be taxed with 20 tons behind the bunker, whilst the staggering total of 80 tons would be brought with ease back along that particular section; another level of euphoria had been reached. The engine was called *Buckingham* and, after suggestions by Jones regarding the rather small firebox and various modifications, a second engine was purchased for the line. It appears that this purchase, rather than hire, was instructed by the agents for the Tramway, Chaplin & Horne; this was on 28th December 1877. Although somewhat circumspect, the fact that the agency of Chaplin & Horne was

(Above): Although the quality of this print is much less than desirable, it does provide a unique view, not of the Manning Wardle locomotive and the train, but of the track layout. Modellers, especially, please note the track in the foreground, running alongside the cattle dock and into the first locomotive shed on the extreme left. This track runs parallel with the cattle dock, and not away from it, as the relaid track of the Metropolitan eventually did.
J. C. Barnes

(Centre): A diagram of the layout of the station at Brill, during the survey for the line to Oxford in 1883. Although the layout of the lines can be accepted as authentic, there is, in the drawing, a measure of simplification. Nevertheless, it does give a good indication of how the Wotton Tramway looked before the alterations to the track layout, first of all by the Oxford & Aylesbury Railway, and then further by the Metropolitan. The centre rectangle, No. 23, is the original train shed terminus. Shed No. 27 was built to store and maintain rolling stock, whilst the small building, with the short siding running into it, was the first locomotive shed. A water tank was put alongside this in October 1877.
Oxford County Council

(Bottom): Rarely illustrated, this scene, photographed by J. C. Barnes of Brill, in the late nineteenth century, affords a glimpse of the station as operated by the O&AT, showing the low platform and light tramway track. For a company of slender financial resources, it is noticeable that it did not seek further revenue by the almost Fauvist display of poster advertising that clamoured from many station billboards during this period. As other photographs will show, it certainly crept in during later years alongside the timetables. Many examples of the genre did, in fact, achieve the distinction of fine art.

J. C. Barnes

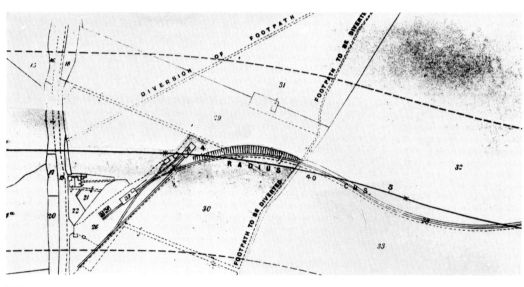

terminated by the Duke a few days later, 31st December, and the line and its dealings was taken on by himself, suggests the probability that the Duke was not altogether in agreement with this recent purchase. That being as it may, Jones was delighted to have the engines and *Wotton* replaced the former engine after some repairs and modifications in mid-March 1878. In the following May, he was to state that, 'The engine is working very well and doing all of the work, with a trip once or twice by the other engine to Kingswood.' This suggests that one of the Aveling Porters was traversing the Kingswood branch to the coal wharf and Yeat Farm Siding where they delivered cattle cake, as the former hired engine *Buckingham* was returned to Bagnalls at the end of March. This hire had cost the Tramway £600 up until August of the previous year, and from that time on until her departure she had been on free hire.

On the subject of the Aveling & Porters, Jones had suggested selling No. 2 as she had proved unaccountably the less reliable of the two. Although the Duke was interested in the prospect of so doing, she must have remained long enough to be sent to the makers in 1881 to have 4ft. 6in. driving wheels fitted, although the precise reason and results of subsequent trials in this form appears to be without documentation.

The Bagnall *Wotton* continued to operate the heavier work on the line for about twenty years and was, in fact, the third and last engine to be purchased by the Wotton Tramway.

The use of rolling stock on the line is as chequered in application as that of the locomotive. From the outset, the Duke had quite reasonably thought of his line as only an agricultural railway, but petitions for its use as passenger conveyance prevailed upon him to the extent of expanding its tiny stock of crude unsprung and dumb-buffered 3½ ton trucks with some kind of covered coach. To this purpose, the Duke purchased a four wheel composite carriage from the Ashbury Carriage Company. This spartan vehicle, even for its day, came to exemplify the character of this hedgerow railway, for eventually when its well-worn wheels could no longer follow in the accumulative thousands of miles between Quainton and Brill, it stood immobilised near the lineside at Brill Station, used as a permanent way hut. This vehicle was also supplemented by a horse-drawn tramcar of which, unfortunately, little has come to light, save that it was 14ft. long x 7ft. wide with end-loading balconies, and held 16 to 20 people. Sufficient to say that the riding properties of both vehicles would have required the tolerance of the most hardy passenger, also the most dedicated, for traversing the entire length of the line in about 80 minutes at an average speed of 5m.p.h. At the price of a hard-won shilling (5p) it would be hard put to compete with the working population, who saw little effort in walking ten or twelve miles for nothing. With the use of the locomotives, the horse-drawn tramcar tended to run only on Thursdays when track maintenance and servicing to engines was carried out. Incidental touches of passenger comfort were conceded too, like a monster three gallon kettle that hissed permanently at Brill Station so that a lad could fill footwarmers for the stoic perseverance of Tramway passengers.

At first, the line operated only two trips daily, and a third was added if required. An exception was on Thursday when it seems that only one morning trip was required. During the afternoon, the Aveling & Porter engine was washed out. During the evening a light covered horse-drawn vehicle would take the milk from Wotton to Quainton. When the second Aveling & Porter engine arrived, a regular service of three trains a day could be rostered with four trips on two days of the week. The horse-drawn tramcar was needed only on Thursdays and was

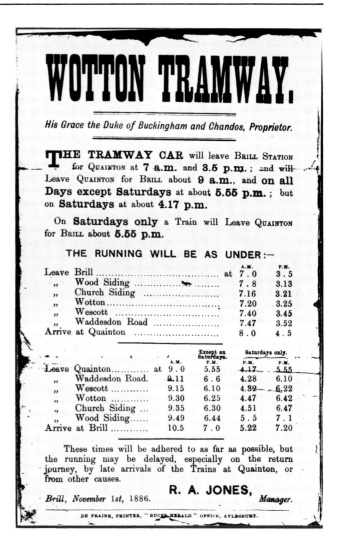

A handbill of November 1886, advertising the service of the horse-drawn Tramcar. The supplementary operation of the car was intended to maintain the connecting service with the A&BR at Quainton. With the exception of one Saturday timing, it was operating a little more than a one hour journey, probably half the time of a brisk walking pace. Use of the Tramcar finally ceased in April 1887.

John Pritchett Collection

kept under a tarpaulin when not in use on the short siding at Wotton Station.

During Wotton Tramway's days, passenger bookings were sparse whilst stock for their accommodation was just about adequate, providing little in the way of comfort. That being said, 104 hardy souls made use of the line in January 1872 and found it satisfactory, for whatever they communicated locally it could not have been unfavourable, as 123 made use of it in the following February and 176 in March, whilst April saw an amazing boost to 224! These figures being regarded in the light of the very sparse population along the line (Westcott 150, Ashendon 300, Wotton 220, Dorton 180 and Brill a virtual metropolis at 1,400) this must appear to be a reasonably encouraging beginning.

This is the only photograph to come to light of the Westcott Gasworks, with its single one-lift holder. Tramway dumb-buffered wagons are evident on the siding. The entrance gate for the rails can be seen in the distance by the side of the retort buildings. Near the far wagon is a pile of coal, whilst the men appear to be barrow loading away a fresh consignment of lime. This was used in the filtration process to remove sulphur. A goat and chickens wandering about is part of the continual reminder of a country railway.

D. Evans Collection

The situation regarding the main purpose of the line, the goods traffic, was, as long as the Tramway could keep its service regular and reliable, one of keen interest. Chaplin & Horne announced, officially, that Wotton Station was open to the conveyance of goods on 1st April 1871 and at Brill Station on 10th May 1872. This was grandly described as being available for access to the lines of the L&NWR and GWR onward to any place in the United Kingdom. For coals, the principle colleries of Warwickshire, Staffordshire, Derbyshire, Leicestershire and South Wales were able to supply. The L&NWR showed particular interest in the burgeoning milk traffic of the area and laid on special vans at Quainton to collect this. This developed to a supply of 5,000 gallons per month which would present considerable activity for the Tramway. Other loads sent from the district were timber, grain and hay. Cattle was brought to the line from Herefordshire, during the spring, and fattened in the district to be despatched at the beginning of winter. Amongst the goods brought in, already mentioned, there were consignments of chalk for the arable clayland to make it more friable; this was known to be ordered in five or six hundred ton loads. Linseed cake for the cattle was also brought in considerable quantities. Coal merchants began to operate their business from all of the railheads, predominantly Wotton and Brill, whilst a coal depot was established at the end of the Kingswood branch and at Church Siding, the latter being for the supply of Wotton House. Obviously, supplies of coal would be needed for the gasworks on the Waddesdon Estate. Rates were generally low on agricultural produce; London manure was carried throughout at 1d (½p) per ton per mile.

For an indication of the financial background to all this, the traffic receipts for the first ten months from March to December 1871 were over £1,000, but could not be accepted as a reflection of normal service, as for the first three months they included movement of goods and minerals during the construction of the line. From January to December 1872, earnings were estimated at £1,400, with £244 earned from goods and minerals and £50 from passenger traffic during the first month. Much of the milk supply in the early days was carried in an 8 ton iron-framed composite carriage, hired from the GWR.

As already mentioned, the requirements of signalling on the line were sparse. Much communication was made by use of the electric telegraph which was installed in 1872 with instruments at Brill, Wotton, Waddesdon and Quainton Road. Occupation of the line was monitored by the use of a train staff; Quainton to Wotton — blue, Wooton to Brill — red, with a special staff being issued from Wotton for the Kingswood branch, also red. Semaphore signals were significant by their absence. The only signals at Quainton were for the entrance and departure from the branch to the main line, when a complete junction was built. After that, there was a rudimentary device installed at Wotton for protecting the use of the Kingswood branch. This consisted of two semaphores erected at the junction for each line which were slotted with a starter signal at the end of the Wotton platform. When this was pulled off, it cleared the road through to the branch blocking the main line. After leaving Wooton, the guard of the train alighted when the junction had been cleared, and returned the signal to danger, releasing the main line and sealing off the Kingswood branch. This action would also return the signal at Wotton which would inform the staff there that the train had now cleared the line.

A prospect of Brill as a spa was an enterprise that would certainly have stimulated development of the Tramway, as well as local trade. A beneficent spring of chalybeate water, between Dorton and Brill, was remarked upon by Queen Victoria on her visit to Waddesdon in 1890. Sufficient optimism for such prospects were aroused in the form of a pump house and bath, with plans for local houses being the recipients of the many invalid and infirm that would descend on the neighbourhood. In the event Brill's prospect shrank to become Cheltenham's reality, as the Queen decided to enoble the latter venue, and speculators withdrew from the disconsolate weed and ivy strewn ruins of neo-classical grandeur in the woods twixt Dorton and Brill. Jones looked all ways to develop the Tramway's potential but seemed each time snared by an uncanny resistance to developments in the area. The fact that the Duke was abroad most of the time, as President of Madras, must have left him somewhat isolated after dispensing of the services of Chaplin & Horne.

Part of the Achilles' heel of his position was the necessity for good relations with the parent line, the Aylesbury & Buckingham Railway, across whose metals much of the Tramway traffic had to pass to reach the L&NWR at Verney Junction and the GWR at Aylesbury. It was essential that good working agreements were established with this company which was, alas, not the case. The problems seem to have risen through personal confrontation between Jones and his opposite number on the A&BR, J. G. Rowe, Secretary and Traffic Manager. Rowe seems to have found the Tramway something of an irritation, and pressured Jones on the subject of division of rates by trying to exact rather more than the Tramway could economically afford, especially with regard to the lucrative milk traffic. Rowe thought that the Tramway should be charged at the rate for conveying beyond Quainton, whereas Jones felt that the charge should be the Quainton Road only rate. Whether Rowe was simply being conscientious to secure the best terms for his own company, which was by no means profitable, or whether he felt some personal spite for the attendant line is difficult to be certain. What is evident is that the two men did not see eye to eye, which ill served the patrons of the Tramway. Milk missed connections and became unsaleable, forcing Jones to complain personally to the Duke who was the Chairman of the larger concern and owner of the smaller. He reiterated Rowe's statement that he would not take milk unless there was an increase in price to the sender, Tramway senders being in default compared to other senders in the district, which would quite naturally draw senders to the Tramway. During one very heated exchange, personal violence was threatened and the men parted on the very worst terms imaginable. This resulted in Jones having to arrange for all the milk to be unloaded at Waddesdon Station and sent by road to the milk factory at Aylesbury, which must have been of great inconvenience to the Tramway, both financially and as a working arrangement. The feud was still active as late as September 1888, when Rowe blocked the telegraph along the Tramway and would never answer letters regarding the same. The fact that Rowe was also singlehandedly managing the Watlington Railway probably did not help his temper.

Jones showed himself to be an efficacious Manager by trying to place as much business as possible under the Tramway's control. He hired carriers to operate local village rounds centred on the nearest railhead. This was so successful that he bought a cart and employed a Tramway carrier. The carrier was kept well occupied and operated the district in turn through the week, starting with Dorton, Pollicott, Ludgershall, Ashendon and Piddington to Brill on Mondays and Thursdys. The Wotton round to Boarstall, Little London, Oakley and Gravel Pits was on Tuesdays and Fridays. Further along the line, at Westcott, he would visit Ham Green, Kingswood, Grendon Underwood and Edgcott on Wednesdays and Saturdays.

The first financial year of the Tramway's operation showed up well its usefulness, as by the last day of March 1873 it had achieved a working profit of £1,002. However, this was followed by an unfortunate period of derailments and breakdowns which tended to undermine local confidence. Also, the rancorous Rowe took advantage of the helpless position of the Tramway coal rates and increased them by 6d. (2½p) a ton, which Jones was afraid to pass on, as the Bicester railhead of the L&NWR was beginning to draw some merchants away. The Aylesbury & Buckingham Railway's position between the Tramway and its access to the larger companies around it was constricting, as arrangements go, as the A&BR would not accept any through rates, but exacted the full parliamentary toll on traffic with ordinary rates of whichever company's line it needed to reach on either end of the A&BR.

However, to give some indication of the amount of mileage being run on the line in the year 1878 when, for a short period, the line had the use of four locomotives, here are the tabulated details:

7,220 trucks hauled 25,676 miles
840 milk vans hauled 3,396 miles
28 horse-boxes hauled 164 miles
2,180 carriages hauled 13,374 miles

Total 10,268   42,610 miles

Locomotive commitment during that same year was as follows:

Engine	120 ran	12,268 miles	*Wotton*
Engine	2 ran	1,071 miles	Aveling Porter 846
Engine	1 ran	104 miles	Aveling Porter 807
Engine	16 ran	963 miles	*Buckingham*

Total 14,406 miles

The success of the Bagnall *Wotton* is self evident, and even *Buckingham* that operated for only just over a month in this year had a comparably high mileage. The puny efforts of the Aveling Porter engines, particularly No. 1, could be due, in part, to periods out of service through breakdown. Even the plodding horse-drawn tramcar managed to total 508 miles, which was more than its Thursdays only trip from Wotton to Quainton.

The preceding information is an account of the Tramway, for its first twelve years or so, surviving as a short branch from a line that existed as a branch of the GWR-operated Aylesbury line. Both lines were to undergo significant changes through new proprietors. The latter, actually became part of a main line, to some degree fulfilling the hopes of its progenitors. However, in the case of the Brill line, it was the promise of greater things unfulfilled. Had the optimism of Sir Henry Acland, when he spoke of a railway to Brill being of great benefit to the people of Oxford, been borne out by the reality of Brill becoming a spa town, the situation between the two centres of population could have been quite different, with a considerable station at Brill and a line to a third station alongside the River Cherwell at Oxford. The diversification of rail travel in the district is a fascinating conjecture, had this come to pass.

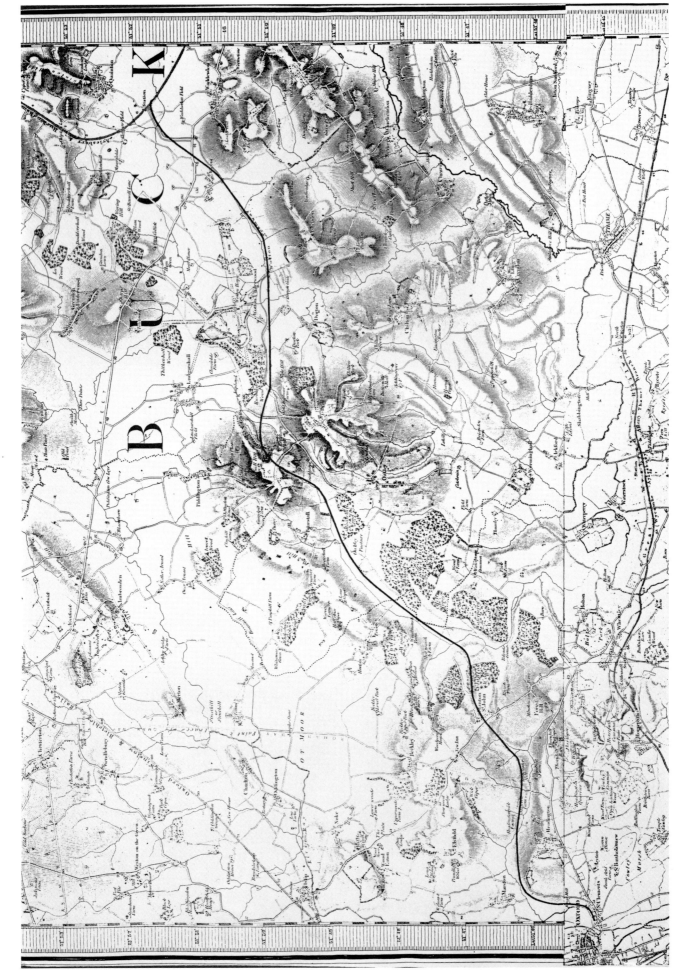

A survey for the Oxford, Aylesbury & Metropolitan Junction Railway, (1883). This included the 1,650 yard tunnel through Muswell Hill. Stations planned from Oxford were as follows: Oxford, Headington, Marston, Stanton St. John, Studley, Boarstall and Brill.

Aylesbury Public Records Office

The Oxford & Aylesbury Tramway

Vintage Metropolitan at Brill, with a Manning Wardle engine and an Oldbury stock coach; note 'MR' on the buffer beam of the locomotive. Although bullhead rail has been installed, the platform has not yet been reconstructed from its mid-age condition. The men of Brill seemed to take regular photographic calls, and seemed to enter with some enthusiasm to the appreciative camera. Men known on this picture are Harry Cross, looking from the cab, with possibly Arthur Bayliss, fireman, on the left side of the engine smokebox. On the other side is Jack Lewis with Tom Cook, Harry Wheeler and the slightly reticent governor, Stationmaster James Hilsden.

Lens of Sutton

The Duke of Buckingham and Sir Edward Watkin developed a great deal of rapport in their railway interests, and appeared to have communicated freely on their plans and hopes for railway developments since the Buckinghamshire Railway days. Watkin's energies had, up until the 1880s, been directed in pushing the newly-developed London Metropolitan Railway northwards, apparently hoping to develop a trunk line scheme. From what moment the embryo of his thinking perceived it as part of the great transcontinental line from Lancashire, through the channel tunnel to Paris, it is not easy to say, save that by the time that he had managed to push the Metropolitan Railway from Rickmansworth to Aylesbury in 1892, and discussed with the Duke the absorption of the Aylesbury & Buckingham Railway, it was obvious that he was not merely seeking to extend the Metropolitan Railway to Verney Junction. For a period of time Watkin became Chairman of the A&BR.

It is therefore no coincidence that the Duke should syndicate two other principle landowners, the untiring Sir Harry Verney and the more recent Baron Ferdinand de Rothschild, to promote a new railway — the Oxford, Aylesbury & Metropolitan Junction Railway. It was to be the only time that these three great families joined in a railway scheme, which rather sharpened the irony of its failure.

The company was formed on 30th November 1882. A line was to be built to main line standards, a single set of rails laid down at first, with provision for another set to be laid alongside. It would be 17 miles 4 furlongs and 8 chains in length, starting from a new junction with the Aylesbury & Buckingham line, south of the Tramway whose connection it virtually ignored. In

its chosen path it continued to do the same, except where it could not reasonably follow another route. The obvious reason for this being that the line, to be laid out as a conventional railway, would require easier curves to allow for faster timings that would be essential to run a successful service. To what degree the stations would be allocated along the Tramway area was never ascertained. Quainton and Brill were obvious places that would remain but, in all probability, much of the existing Tramway stops would be worked out to one or two intermediate stations. There are some clues of the intentions of the company beyond Brill with a station for Boarstall, Stanton St. John and Horton, with another one at the site of Wick Farm, near Headington. Finally on the eastern bank of the River Cherwell at York Place in St. Clements, Oxford, there would be another terminus station. The scheme was perfectly feasible and may well have come to fruition had there not been one very serious obstacle, and this was the prospect of having to tunnel through Muswell Hill, near Brill. As surveyed, this would require a bore of 1,650 yards and a very hard prospect for the promoters of the line. The Duke stated that the new line would make the route between Aylesbury and Oxford a distance of 23 miles as compared with the 28 miles on the GWR and 34 miles on the L&NWR. The rafters of the Sun Inn, Brill, resounded to the approval of a public meeting held there on 2nd March 1883.

The Bill received the Royal Assent on 20th August 1883. Interestingly, a clause was inserted referring to special permission being required from the President and scholars protecting the land and properties of St. Mary Magdalen College on the site called Kings Mill. Working capital was set at £300,000, divided into £10 shares. The existing Wotton Tramway that operated along some of the route was virtually ignored, save for a protective clause in the Act which stated that, where interfering with the Wotton Tramway, a separate line of rails would be laid so that the tramway could continue its business, and also, before interfering with the same, was a clause to purchase the line from the Duke of Buckingham if he so wished. In view of the Duke's involvement in the new railway, it can be reasonably assumed that, when the new line was open, the Tramway would cease to exist.

The fact that sufficient capital was not generated within the five years of the powers of the Act must hinge on a number of conflicting factors. The line did not have the direct financial support of one of the larger companies, and it makes great sway of working arrangements with the GWR at Quainton over the A&BR, but the Metropolitan Railway's northern advance can be viewed with no little suspicion. At the same time the Metropolitan Railway were not actively supporting a railway to Oxford. Another factor that must have been cautious to finance was the risky undertaking of tunnelling. Early railway speculation had been reckless by comparison and soon found, to its cost, that large engineering works, especially tunnels, could turn into bottomless pits that swallowed money and spread ruin, whilst the possibility of Brill's expansion was probably viewed by a wait-and-see conclusion by many investors, which, in the event, proved to be justified. Whatever, the line was not started, not a blade of grass disturbed, and the Tramway continued to hobble on.

Not to be entirely dissuaded from seeing it through, the promoters modified their prospectus and drew up a second Bill which was submitted under the title, 'Oxford & Aylesbury Tramroad'; this was now quite another matter. It was no longer seen at the outset as a fast double track connecting route, but as an extension to what was virtually an agricultural line, admittedly easing some of the curves of the existing Tramway line whilst the extension of 11 miles 4 chains and 50 links joined end-on with the line at Brill. The avoidance of a tunnel by going between Muswell and Brill hills was, without question, the most significant difference in the survey.

This second Bill received the Royal Assent on 7th August 1888. An Agreement dated from 17th July, previous scheduled to this Act, provided for the new company to rent or buy the Wotton Tramway. Amongst the other differences to the line was the station at Oxford. This would now be in George Street, St. Clements, a little further away from Magdalen Bridge. What must be regarded with some reserve on this proposal is the 18 miles; a lengthy route to serve on the Tramway system, remembering all that had so far come amiss on the existing short section of line, not to mention the speed limit of some 12 m.p.h. It was obvious that, for the line to work properly at all, the short-comings of the existing section would have to be overcome with substantial transverse sleepers and better track. Authorised capital for the Act was set at £100,000; ten thousand shares of £10 each.

The first Manning Wardle engine to be employed on the line was a K type, built in 1876. It was delivered new to T. J. Waller of Manchester and given the name *Prestwich* on 28th July of that year. After passing through the hands of one or more owners, before reaching J. D. Newell of Todmorden who named it *Huddersfield*, which was painted on the tank sides and is faintly visible on this photograph, the engine passed into the hands of the Oxford & Aylesbury Tramway, around September 1894. This was after it had finished its work on the construction of the Edington to Bridgwater line of the Somerset & Dorset Joint Railway in 1890. Details of the locomotive are as follows: Works No. 616, inside cylinders 12in. x 17in. stroke. Resting on 3ft. diameter driving wheels is the weight of 18 tons, across a base of 10ft. 9in. Contrary to the appearance on this photograph, the engine is an 0-6-0 saddle tank. Whatever the reason for removing the front section of the coupling rod is not clear. In view of the nature of the Brill line, it is quite possible that the releasing of the front wheels, to act as a 2-4-0 bogie arrangement, may have increased the lateral sideplay of the front and reduced derailments. Note the flat bottom rail still in situ at Brill Station in this photograph. The man on the left is said to be Arthur Hilsden, son of Stationmaster James Hilsden.

M. Horne Collection

The tramway assembly, about 1900. Alongside the new station at Quainton, standing on freshly ballasted bullhead rail, *Huddersfield* waits to leave for Brill. Slight protection for the men is the weatherboard and canvas cover pinned to the leading coach. The first coach is the original Wotton Tramway coach of 1872 vintage. It had a 9ft. wheelbase, 22ft. 6in. over frame, and 25ft. 10in. over buffers; the width was 17ft. 1in. over the body. The second curiosity in the rake is one of the Pair of Bristol Carriage & Wagon Co. open saloon stock, a tramway style coach, in fact. The last wagon requires little description with its collection of conical milk churns.

London Transport Executive

In the same year, a Mr Pain, representing the contractors Baldry & Yerburgh, gave an estimate for the rebuilding of the line, re-laying track and rebuilding stations for £10,728. Not surprisingly, Jones considered that such expenditure could not be justified in the light of existing Tramway returns. Nevertheless, reconstruction was agreed, but could not begin until shortly after 14th February 1894, with the Tramway trying to continue business as best it could whilst this took place. The delay was due yet again to the want of investment, and the Act fared no better than the previous one, probably for different reasons, amongst them being that it was really too great a compromise from the former unsupported ideal through sparsely populated countryside. What would next count against the wavering investment was the death of the Duke of Buckingham on 26th March 1889. It meant the loss of a great railway figure in the area and was the kind of set-back that could seriously affect sensitive capital investment. Nevertheless, the promoters applied for and were granted an Act of Extension on 27th June 1892. This was to extend the period for starting work on the line up until 17th August 1894, and also to deviate between Stanton St. John and Brill further to join the Tramway 31 chains from the terminus. Again, the runes were cast against this company when another fateful blow was struck in their progress by the death of Sir Harry Verney of Claydon House, on Monday, 12th February 1894. He, like the Duke, had featured so prominently in many local railway schemes. Thus in a few years, the men directly responsible for exerting the greatest influence in railway matters had left the scene.

Fulfilling the stipulation of the Act, the Oxford & Aylesbury Tramroad took over the Wotton Tramway from 1st April 1894. Reconstruction had been underway since the preceding February, and the company asked Earl Temple, heir to the Duke of Buckingham, if he would continue to work the line until the reconstruction was complete and approved by the

(Below):   A drawing of the Bristol Carriage & Wagon Company coach bought for use on the Tramway by the OA&T. The end balconies, steps and diamond bogies tend to emphasise the 'frontier' characteristics of American appearance. Dimensions were 30ft. long over body, and 7ft. 6in. wide. The steel underframes were mounted on two four wheel bogies and the vehicle was fitted with automatic vacuum brakes. There was accommodation for 40 passengers. The drawing is in the popular modelling scale of 4mm. to 1ft.

Mike Crosbie

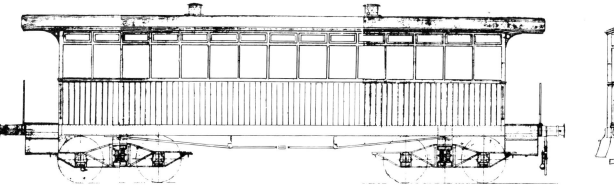
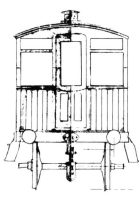

Board of Trade. The company submitted a further Act that was passed on 17th August 1894 for a deviation between Stanton St. John and Brill, where the line would join the Wotton Tramway at a different point, instead of butting end-on, to join the Tramway 30 chains east of Brill Station, avoiding the curved section up to the station. This would, in effect, create a new station site alongside the Brill to Chilton Road. By this time, the prospect of electric traction was to be considered as a possibility, and protective clauses for the Postmaster General were inserted in the Act. Also mentioned in the Act was the Duke's death. This final Act shrunk its working capital still further to £85,000. Although the Wotton Tramway was, none too soon, relaid with new rail and transverse sleepering, capital to extend the line from Brill was never forthcoming. Indeed, the Oxford & Aylesbury Tramroad Company was propped up more than once by assistance from Earl Temple who must, on some occasions, have pondered on his uncle's indulgence from a normally abstemious character, by contrast with his father, by the expense of this little line, for in the Act, by the request of Earl Temple, were the following clauses; it appears that he desired to conclude the estate interest in the enterprise. 'The company shall, within twelve months from the date when £50,000 of the capital have been raised, purchase from the said Earl Temple all rolling stock, fixtures, furniture and stores which at the date of the passing of the Act are the property of Earl Temple and are in use on or about the Wotton Tramway . . . the price to be determined by valuation.' Also, as between Earl Temple and the Company, 'The siding leading from the Wotton Tramway into the works of the Brill Brick Company Limited is and shall remain the property of the Earl Temple, and the Company shall have all reasonable facilities for the interchange of traffic along such sidings from the Tramway authorised by the Act of 1888.'

The inheritance of Earl Temple followed as a result of circumspection of the peerage. When the Duke of Buckingham and Chandos died at the age of 65, he was without male issue, having three daughters by his first wife and no children by his second. One of the daughters, Baroness Kinloss, inherited part of the estate but there was now no living male of the Grenville family, which brought his nephew of the Gore-Langton side of the relations to succeed one of the titles and become Earl Temple of Stowe. It was to him that all of the Wotton Tramway, structures and moveables passed, including the Oxford & Aylesbury Tramway rent, in lieu of acquiring the said capital.

In agreement with the schedule to the Act of 1888, the newly rebuilt line was relaid with 50lb. per yard flat bottom rail, spiked to transverse sleepering with flange bolts, dog spikes and sole plates. The lengths were fished at the joints. More obviously of benefit for the passengers on the line was the provision of firm platforms, waiting-rooms and lavatories alongside the ticket offices at all the stations, with the exception of Wood Siding. After the early excursion from that point, it is doubtful whether this minor station would be called upon for much passenger traffic, more often serving the duties of a goods siding. Therefore, all that was constructed at this spot was a corrugated hut shelter for the man on duty from which tickets were issued later. Its paucity can well be appreciated in the dimensions in the plan of 9ft. x 6ft. Hopefully, the line would now be able to shake off the chagrin of persistent derailments; certainly on the main line. In the case of the Kingswood branch, this was not rebuilt with new rail as there was no justification at all for the expense. Earl Temple allowed the company to retain this at a peppercorn rent of £1 per year. After Mr G. Herbert Peake, Chairman of the Oxford & Aylesbury Tramway, carried out an

examination of the line in October 1894, he stated that the line was well maintained. The branch was leased from 31st December of the same year for 21 years, with optional reversions at 7 and 14 years. It did, however, manage to run the full course and expired some time just after the outbreak of World War I. At the time of the agreement there were two coal merchants operating from the end of the branch, a Mr Humphreys and Mr J. T. Oxley; the latter gentleman was, in fact, the agent to Earl Temple who would be registered at coal wharves elsewhere on the system.

In order to perform a more businesslike relationship with through traffic, the Oxford & Aylesbury Tramway began, from the outset, to subscribe the business of the line to the Railway Clearing House and its regulations. This approach necessitated the speedy despatch of the two Aveling Porter locomotives to Nether Heyford Brickworks in Northamptonshire, on 23rd September 1895, to be replaced be an engine design that had been popularly used by railway building contractors on their lightly laid temporary railways. The obvious advantage of this Manning Wardle K class 0-6-0 locomotive, *Huddersfield*, besides being a more powerful and altogether more workmanlike machine, was its exceptionally light axle loading of 6 tons per axle, although a little in excess of the Tramway limit of 5 tons per axle; a sensitive point for engines employed on the Brill Tramway.

When delivered new to T. J. Waller of Manchester in 1876, the engine carried the name *Prestwich*. On passing to another owner, J. D. Newell of Todmorden, it was rechristened with her trans-Pennine name *Huddersfield*, which first hears mention in this corner of leafy Buckinghamshire in September 1894.

Not only to have new station facilities and travel behind faster engines, but the passengers were also about to have the facility of travelling in roomier carriages, bought from the Bristol Carriage and Wagon Co., in 1895, thus enabling a more presentable composite train to be formed, although the original four wheel composite was not to end her days yet, for this vehicle was to remain in service and was freshly painted and lettered in the new company's name and livery. All of this restorative activity followed in the wake of the all important inspection by an officer of the Board of Trade, who came to inspect the line after its reconstruction.

On 19th October 1894, Major General C. S. Hutchinson, RE inspected the works of the newly-reconstructed Wotton Tramway. In his report, he noted that the line had a short gradient of 1 in 36 (very short) and others of 1 in 39, 1 in 40 and 1 in 41 beside a curve of 6¾ chains at Quainton, curves of 9½ chains at Brill, and two other curves of 10 chains and 13 chains. In conclusion, he found that the line was satisfactory for its light tramway traffic, but added that there were four level crossing places of the public road without statutory sanction. These had, in fact, been approved by the Buckinghamshire County Council on the stipulation that the gates remained in the normal position; open for the highway. Nevertheless, the inspecting engineer felt that these should be legalised in the next Bill (1894). He stated that there was no proper rolling stock, only a contractors engine which was a tramway type car and a brake van. Traffic had, however, been safely conducted with this rolling stock for the past 22 years. He also stated that there were no under or overbridges, which was, at that time, true, as the GCR bridge at Wotton and the GWR bridge at Wood Siding were still events of the future. He felt that should the proposed extension to Oxford be undertaken, the line should be operated on the electric train staff or the staff and ticket system, with block signalling.

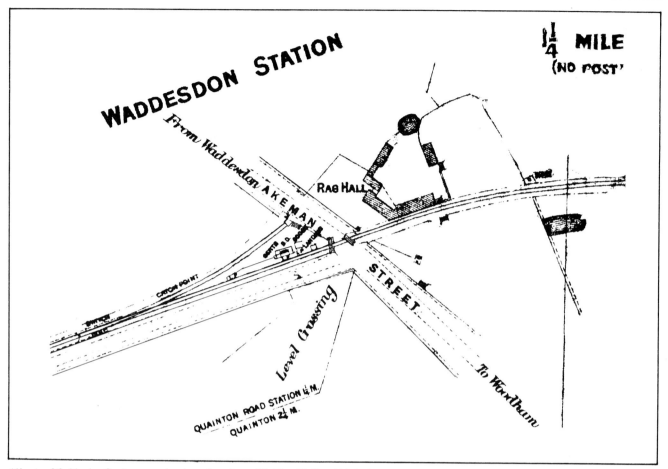

(Above): Waddesdon Station, or as locals preferred to call it 'Rag Hall', which is the name of the farm on the other side of the road. In Wotton Tramway days, there was but a single siding at this place and nothing else, save the crossing gates that opened to allow the line to cross the historical Akeman Street, a Roman route from St. Albans to Bath.

Mike Crosbie

An undertaking, dated 22nd November 1894, was given by Messrs G. Herbert Peake and D. Navone, both Directors, and H. H. M. Smith, Secretary under the Seal of the Oxford & Aylesbury Tramroad Company, to supply within 6 months, such rolling stock as might be necessary to comply with Schedule 1 of the Company's Act of 1888. There was also an undertaking to secure parliamentary sanction to the public road level crossings and restrict the speed limit to 12m.p.h. with 8m.p.h. at the crossings and 4m.p.h. on the journey between Wotton and Brill at Thame Lodge Crossing.

Although the company rebuilt the track, bought better rolling stock and engines, they were never able to raise sufficient money to obtain the freehold of the line, nor did they take steps to secure parliamentary sanction for the public road crossings. With regard to locomotives, the second-hand purchase of the Manning Wardle, *Huddersfield*, was improved further with the purchase of a brand new K class engine from the Boyne Engine Works, Leeds, which was delivered on the 5th December 1894. This was paid for with Lloyd's Bonds. When The Oxford & Aylesbury Tramroad Company could not meet the Bonds, Earl Temple had, not for the first time nor the last, to step in and help the company by buying the engine outright for the sum of £1,000 and renting it to the company at £2 per week. The fact that to comply with the regulations under the Act it was to be

fitted with a governor for a 12m.p.h. speed limit, added a further £40 to the the cost. The works number of the engine was 1249 and it was understandably called *Earl Temple*, although later it was renamed *Brill No. 1*. An obvious difference between the two Manning Wardle engines was that *Earl Temple* had a proper roof over the footplate, whilst the elder *Huddersfield* was fitted only with a weatherboard and canvas cover. Whether or not *Huddersfield* was ailing, when purchased, or suffered further on the Tramway, it was a matter of only twelve months later, in 1895, that she required urgent repairs and had to be taken out of service. Until the purchase of a third engine from the same manufacturers, *Earl Temple* continued to run the service. On 7th February 1899, this third K class engine was delivered, Works No. 1415, to be named *Wotton No. 2*, the first *Wotton* having been the Bagnall engine of Wotton Tramway days, which appears to have been sold with the arrival of *Huddersfield*.

In 1895, the Tramway first appeared in Railway Clearing House returns for goods and parcel traffic, which facilitated the through booking of freight. Passenger bookings were not given. An unfortunate oversight was to have the Tramway waybills closely similar in appearance to those of the L&NWR, which caused the little railway's merchandising to be abstracted and accounted as that of the latter.

The Manning Wardle engines took four trains each way at a

OXFORD & AYLESBURY TRAMROAD.

NOVEMBER, 1899, and until further Notice.

WEEK DAYS ONLY.

STATIONS.	A.M.	A.M.	P.M.	P.M.
BRILL..............dpt.	8.10	10.30	3.5	5.15
WOOD SIDING .... ,,	8.19	10.38	3.13	5.23
WOTTON .... ,,	8.30	10.48	3.23	5.33
WESTCOTT .... ,,	8.40	10.57	3.32	5.42
WADDESDON .... ,,	8.45	11.0	3.35	5.45
QUAINTON ....arr.	8.53	11.10	3.45	5.55
QUAINTON (Met.)...dpt.	9.22	11.22	3.57	6.22
AYLESBURY ,, ...arr.	9.35	11.35	4.10	6.35
BAKER STREET ,, ...arr.	11.8	1.8	5.43	8.8
AYLESBURY (Joint)..dpt.	10.10	11.50	4.49	7.0
PADDINGTON (G.W.) arr.	12.40	2 10	6.45	9.30
AYLESBURY (L.N.W.) dpt.	11.10	12.57	5.15	7.30
EUSTON ,, ...arr.	12.40	4.0	8.35	9.15
QUAINTON (Met.)......dpt.	9.52	12.18	4.13	6.2
VERNEY ,, ...arr.	10.9	12.33	4.30	6.18
BUCKINGHAM(L.N.W.) ,,	11.4	1.25	5.11	7.15
BANBURY (*Thur. only) ,,	*11.55	2.5	5.52	8.15
OXFORD (L.N.W.) ...arr.	11.30	3.15	5.30	8.0
BLETCHLEY ,, ... ,,	10.55	1.5	5.46	8.36
EUSTON ,, ... ,,	12.40	2.45	7.35	10.25

STATIONS.	A.M.	A.M.	P.M.	P.M.
EUSTON (L.N.W.)...dpt.	7.10	8.45	12.25	2.45
BLETCHLEY ,, ... ,,	8.30	10.20	2.5	4.30
OXFORD ,, ... ,,	7.50	9.50	2.25	4.50
BANBURY ,, ... ,,	7.35	9.50	2.35	4.25
BUCKINGHAM ,, ... ,,	8.24	10.28	3.10	5.14
VERNEY (Met.)... ,,	9.5	11.5	3.40	6.5
QUAINTON ,, ...arr.	9.22	11.22	3.57	6.22
PADDINGTON (G.W.)..dpt.	...	9.15	11.15	2.0
AYLESBURY (Joint) ...arr.	...	11.25	1.20	4.8
EUSTON (L.N.W.) ...dpt.	...	9.10	1.45	3.0
AYLESBURY ,, ...arr.	...	10.57	3.32	5.5
BAKER STREET (Met.)dpt.	*6.9	10.27	2.27	4.17
*Change at Neasden				
AYLESBURY ,, ...dpt.	7.51	12.5	4.0	5.49
QUAINTON ,, ...arr.	8.4	12.18	4.13	6.2
QUAINTON ....dpt.	9.30	12.25	4.15	6.25
WADDESDON .... ,,	9.40	12.35	4.23	6.33
WESTCOTT .... ,,	9.43	12.38	4.26	6.36
WOTTON .... ,,	9.53	12.47	4.36	6.46
WOOD SIDING .... ,,	10.2	12.57	4.43	6.53
BRILL ....arr.	10.10	1.5	4.50	7.0

Trains will only stop at Waddesdon, Westcott, and Wood Siding by Signal, or for Passengers to alight, &c.

R. A. JONES. *General Manager.*

G. T. DE FRAINE, PRINTER, "BUCKS HERALD" OFFICE, WALTON STREET, AYLESBURY.

(Above): The Tramway timetable in the year of the opening of the Great Central Railway, operating four trains on forty minute journeys, with only Wotton as a mandatory stopping point en route. There is ample time at Quainton for through connections, whilst at this high point of the railway age, diverse routes abound.

M. Horne Collection

speed not exceeding 12m.p.h. None of the trains were compelled to stop at any station except Wotton and were all classified as mixed trains, with the early Wotton Tramway coach still attached at one end of the train, together with one of the new bogie coaches and a low-sided goods wagon for carrying the shuttle of milk churns back and forth along the line. During the operating period of the O&AT, there were four train journeys each way daily on a time of 40 minutes.

Confidence in the administration of R. A. Jones was reinforced by his position on the Board as General Manager. For a brief period he was Managing Director, but resigned this position in December 1896 to remain simply as Manager with a salary of £250 per annum. It must have been with some relief for the ageing custodian when the company installed a telephone from the station at Brill to the Tramway offices in the village, which was also his home; 'The Grove' on the High Street.

Another position to alter in 1895 was that of Chairman, which was occupied by Earl Temple himself on 4th November.

In order to comply with Schedule 1 of the Act of 1888, the company was obliged to review the passenger coach situation. In consequence, they ordered two tramway type coaches from the Bristol Carriage & Wagon Co., in February 1895. A bond finance of £641 was again rescued by Earl Temple. The coaches were 30ft. over body and 7ft. 6in. wide; they had continuous side windows and were canopied at both ends. In a single saloon, they seated a total of forty passengers, arranged in seats along each side of the vehicle. As can be readily appreciated from photographs, being designed for tramway use they were of very light construction, with steel underframes and diamond frame bogies with cast steel spoke wheels. However, at least they did comply with contemporary braking regulations by having automatic vacuum brakes; quite a development for the Brill line.

Passenger services under the new régime omitted Church Siding from the timetable for the first time. In 1895, a grand total of four trains each way daily was announced, taking forty to forty three minutes to get from Quainton to Brill, whilst the return trip was more speedily accomplished in thirty five to thirty eight minutes. After a brief period of three trips only, the best service that the line had ever seen was achieved by the following April, with four daily trips once more becoming the norm. Not to rest on its laurels, by May 1897 no fewer than five daily journeys in both directions were being accomplished; a two-hourly service with one four hour gap. As an obvious adjuct to the main line, the trains connected with the services from Aylesbury to Verney Junction at Quainton Road. These were operated on a two hour basis connecting with the one hour service from Aylesbury to Baker Street. To be success-

A view from the end of Westcott Station Siding around the turn of the century, still with light Tramway track upon which one of the Manning Wardle engines is making a bunker first trip 'up' the line. In the train of one empty wagon and coach with tumble-home ends, is a large sheeted load. The liberal use of canvas covering for wagons is a point worth mentioning for modellers, especially concerning the Brill line.

S. W. A. Newton/Leicester County Council

A view of the entrance to Wotton Station on the Tramway during the 1930s. The road curving around the tree to the right is to the coal drop and stables. The building on the right is the yard side of the goods shed; the milk landing being alongside it. The main station building is in the centre of the picture, with the platform unseen on its rail side. Posts of fencing to the left are confused with remains of the cattle dock fencing, whilst in the left foreground is the raised end-loading ramp. The siding to this was the one extended during the construction of the other Wotton Station of the GWR & GCR Joint.

London Transport Executive

A view through the woods near Wood Siding, showing light Tramway track and the characteristic post and wire fencing. The telegraph poles, in fact, belonged to the Post Office and carried three wires. Two of these were rented to the Tramway, whilst a third was the Post Office connection between Waddesdon and Brill. This moment of evening sunlight was captured by Newton some eighty years ago.

S. W. A. Newton/Leicester County Council

In acknowledgement to the memory of that much travelled railway photographer, S. W. A. Newton, this photograph, along with many others, provides a unique glimpse of how the Tramway looked around the turn of the century. The magnificent photographic record, compiled by Newton, of the construction of the London Extension of the Manchester, Sheffield & Lincolnshire Railway, is justly famous. It is due to his copious following of this work that he recorded the work of the GWR/GCR Joint link line from Grendon Underwood to Ashendon; this included the new Wotton Station, not forgetting the one already there. Turning his camera beyond the fence, this view is looking down from the new embankment. On the siding leading to the goods shed are two of the Tramway's 3½ ton dumb-buffered wagons. Included is a rare observation of the coal siding across the picture in the foreground. Possibly part of the colony of temporary wooden huts for the construction gangs is visible on the left, whilst in the foreground is one of the familiar side-tipping spoil wagons, so familiar on railway construction, being drawn along contractors' lines behind horses. Mechanisation in view are the hand-operated winches, probably used for hauling timbers and scaffolding for the construction of the railway overbridge.

S. W. A. Newton/Leicester County Council

Another Newton print, closely related in time to the previous one, if not the same day, showing the new plate girder bridge over the Tramway. Also visible is the Tramway light profile flat bottom rail, which was used in the period between the original bridge rail and the eventual bullhead rail installed by the Metropolitan.

Leicester Museum

ful, therefore, the Tramway had to maintain its connection in the chain. In order to try and fill its new coaches, the O&AT daringly reduced its fare from one shilling (5p) to 6½d. (3p) single, hoping that this would attract passengers who probably felt that the service had been somewhat overpriced. Intermediate fares had odd half pennies with the curiosity, for a short time, of retaining the farthing; the only line in the country to do so. The fare from Quainton to Wood Siding was 5¾d. (2½p).

Although applying every inducement, the company were not able to attract greater passenger revenue than the average £24 per month, and sustained a net loss of £175 for the year of 1898.

The prospect of the line ever fulfilling its title seemed to rest on the progress of other railway development in the area, which had been gathering momentum from the time when the Metropolitan Railway reached Aylesbury. After their absorption of the Aylesbury & Buckingham Railway on 1st July 1891, the company put in hand extensive works to bring it up to the standards of their existing railway. During the period of rebuilding the Tramway, they approached the Board of the O&AT on the subject of the total resiting of Quainton Road Station, on the southern side of the road crossing. With the doubling of the line to Verney Junction, and the building of the bridge to replace the crossing, it would perforce bring drastic changes to the Tramway's connection to the main line. The actual elevation of the road on to a bridge would sever this connection. One can imagine that the Metropolitan Railway's approach on the subject would be received warmly, as this would, in fact, improve still further connection facilities at Quainton that could only be an advantage to the Tramway, with a proper junction furnished at the Metropolitan Railway's expense, together with the facility of a shared platform with the developing main line service.

By 1895, plans had been put in hand for the rebuilding of the Quainton Station which, when completed, took the form of an 'up' platform facing a wedge-shaped 'down' platform which the Tramway shared.

On 1st January 1897, Quainton Road began with the new Verney Junction to Baker Street service, but still retained the old A&BR service as a shuttle, later worked by a motor train. This meant that one could now travel from Brill and change at Quainton direct for the London terminus.

With the construction of a better connection with the Metropolitan Railway, it would appear that the unfulfilled extension to the City of Oxford might be even more appropriate, but it appears that the lapsed powers of the Act were never resought, even though as late as 1899, the O&AT had not given up hope entirely, but it would require a rather greater interest from the Metropolitan Railway for there to be any prospect of this coming to fruition. By this time, the Metropolitan Railway were embroiled with the nascent development of the Manchester, Sheffield & Lincolnshire Railway's protracted construction of their main line to London, and the uneasy alliance which joined their interests at Quainton Road Station. This, then, would serve as more sufficient a distraction from the unrequited scheme of another terminus at Oxford.

Thus with the Oxford & Aylesbury Tramroad Company counting for little more than a 6¼ mile line from Quainton Road to the attractive, but modest, outpost of Brill village, they felt obliged to give serious thought to what ever terms were available from the Metropolitan Railway Company.

The means by which this transpired is one of the curiosities of railway lore, for it was in the form of a letter to the O&AR Chairman, Earl Temple, from the General Manager of the Metropolitan Railway, Mr John Bell, on behalf of that company, and dated 6th November 1899. Earlier in the year, Bell had corresponded an interest in purchasing the Tramway for £20,000, less the agreed valuation for the rolling stock. In the event a temporary working arrangement with rent at £600 per annum became the norm. Should a purchase be undertaken, it would include the right to double the track at a cost of not more than £100 an acre; this new agreement to be terminated by six months notice on either side. Doubtless, the Metropolitan Railway had decided to keep the line alive, if only for its catchment in milk traffic, whilst keeping their options open if, in the unlikely event, it should prove to be of some value. As events proved, purchase was never required by the Metropolitan Railway, and the line, was, for the period of the lease, worked under the terms of this letter.

Church Siding, after it had been foreshortened to the fence in the distance. Bullhead rail was put in up to this point but, as can be seen from the illustration *(above)*, the old bridge rail and baulk timber was never replaced on the branch. Upturned chairs act as scotch blocks at the end of the siding.

London Transport Executive and S. W. Baker

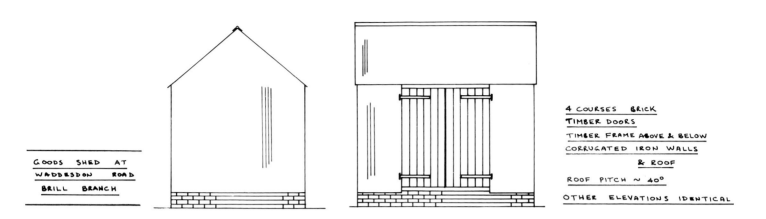

GOODS SHED AT
WADDESDON ROAD
BRILL BRANCH

4 COURSES BRICK
TIMBER DOORS
TIMBER FRAME ABOVE & BELOW
CORRUGATED IRON WALLS
& ROOF
ROOF PITCH ~ 40°
OTHER ELEVATIONS IDENTICAL

Two drawings from the group at Waddesdon; a very minor example of the ubiquitous goods shed, together with a loading platform. These were commonly seen holding milk churns, especially for that early morning train, with the rodeo of farm carts clustering the station area. It is occasionally overlooked that these platforms could sometimes be seen between stations in open country, and an example on the Bletchley to Oxford line is the Charndon Bridge milk stage, between Marsh Gibbon and Claydon stations.

Mike Crosbie

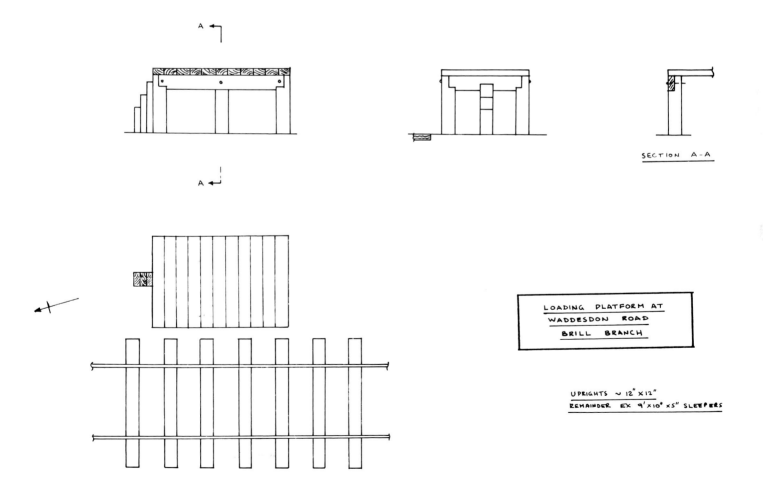

SECTION A-A

LOADING PLATFORM AT
WADDESDON ROAD
BRILL BRANCH

UPRIGHTS ~ 12" X 12"
REMAINDER EX 9' X10° X5" SLEEPERS

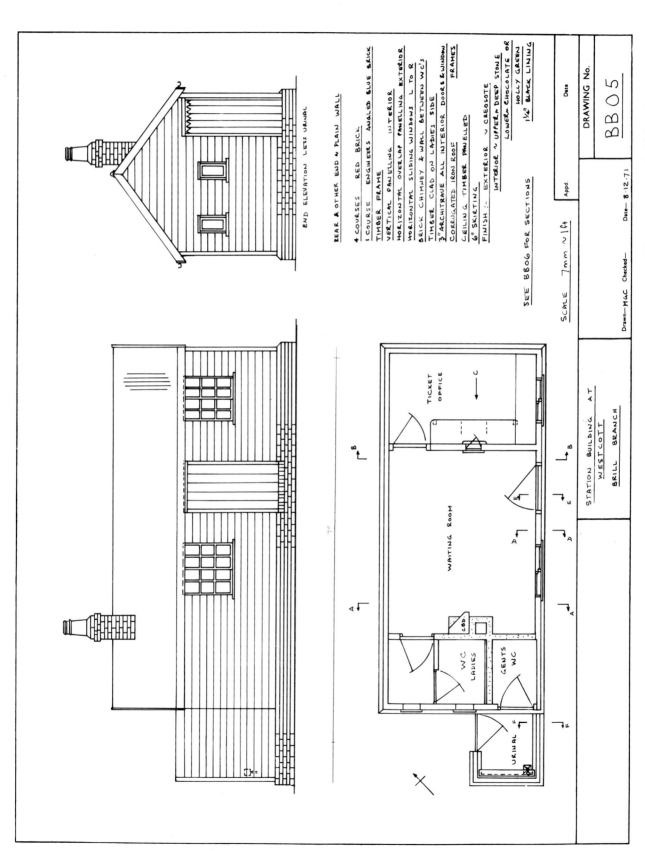

END ELEVATION LETS URINAL

REAR & OTHER END & PLAIN WALL

4 COURSES RED BRICK
1 COURSE ENGINEERS ANGLED BLUE BRICK
TIMBER FRAME
VERTICAL PANELLING INTERIOR
HORIZONTAL OVERLAP PANELLING EXTERIOR
HORIZONTAL SLIDING WINDOWS L TO R
BRICK CHIMNEY & WALL BETWEEN WC'S
TIMBER CLAD ON LADIES SIDE
3" ARCHITRAVE ALL INTERIOR DOORS & WINDOW
                                    FRAMES
CORRUGATED IRON ROOF
CEILING TIMBER PANELLED
6" SKIRTING
FINISH :- EXTERIOR ~ CREOSOTE
     INTERIOR ~ UPPER~ DEEP STONE
          LOWER~ CHOCOLATE OR
               HOLLY GREEN
               1¼" BLACK LINING

SEE BB06 FOR SECTIONS

SCALE 7mm ~|ft

TICKET OFFICE

WAITING ROOM

WC LADIES

GENTS WC

URINAL

STATION BUILDING AT
WESTCOTT
BRILL BRANCH

DRAWING No.

BB05

Date

Appd.

Drawn—M&C Checked— Date—8.12.71

Mike Crosbie

Westcott Station service building, identical to all other stations on the line, the only difference being that this building was constructed with lateral planking, whilst all others were vertical.

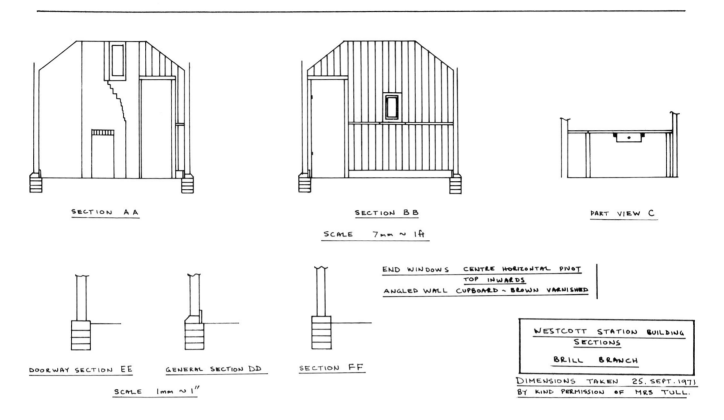

SECTION A A

SECTION B B

PART VIEW C

SCALE   7mm ~ 1ft

DOORWAY SECTION EE

GENERAL SECTION DD

SECTION FF

SCALE   1mm ~ 1"

END WINDOWS   CENTRE HORIZONTAL PIVOT
             TOP INWARDS
ANGLED WALL CUPBOARD ~ BROWN VARNISHED

WESTCOTT STATION BUILDING
       SECTIONS
     BRILL BRANCH

DIMENSIONS TAKEN 25. SEPT. 1971
BY KIND PERMISSION OF MRS TULL.

The entrance to the Brickworks siding, clearly showing the lever and ground signal that made a 45 degree turn as the switch was thrown, turning from green for the main line to white for the siding.

London Transport Executive

(Below):   A diagram of the siding, with loop and storage siding, field gate and switch, before crossing the Brill to Dorton road.

Mike Crosbie

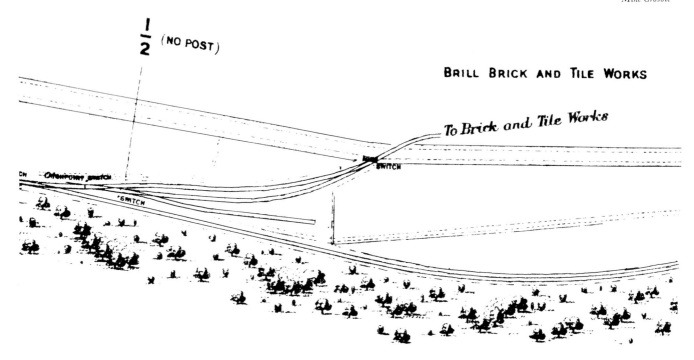

A group of Fenemore's hay-loaders awaiting shipment on the siding loop.

W. E. Fenemore

The arrival of a large consignment of timber baulks on the siding in the works yard, which is beneath the platform where the men are standing.

W. E. Fenemore

Quainton Road, shortly after reconstruction and before the new road bridge replaced the crossing on 11th October 1899. The original signal box is just visible alongside the crossing gates. The site of the new 'up' platform, the other face of which is for Brill trains, has seriously obstructed the view from the box.

S. W. A. Newton/Leicester County Council

Metropolitan tank No. 23 calls at Wotton with a Brill to Quainton train, in the 1930s.

Roy Slaymaker Collection

Two ground plan views of the Westcott Station area. *(Left)* the closer detail of the station, with the gasworks siding leading off through the field gate.*(Right)* the Ordnance Survey showing the entire branch to the retort house and gasholder. Both plans are dated 1900.

Mike Crosbie and Ordnance Survey

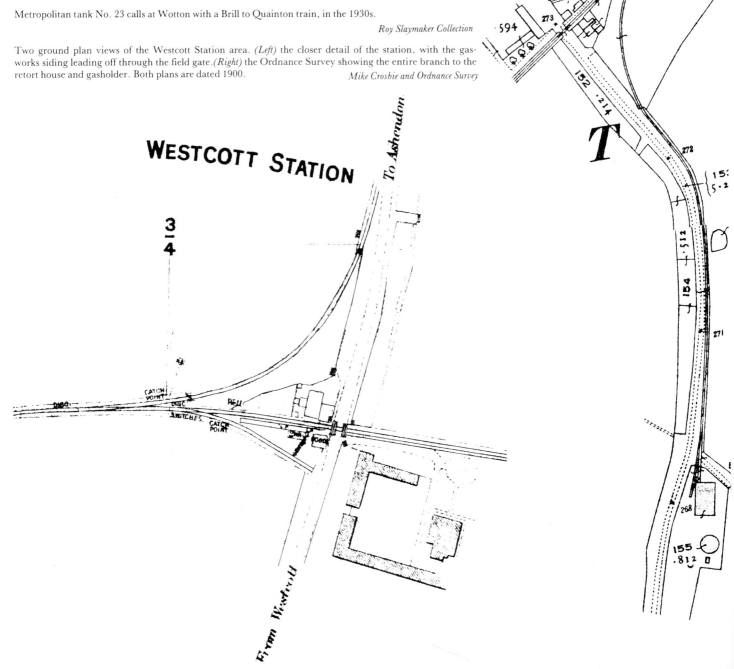

WOTTON STATION

Wotton Station, circa 1910, with the GW&GC Joint line built over the site. At this station, it was possible for a train to use the goods road as a refuge to allow another train to pass. Although the line was worked on a one engine in steam system, or two coupled together, this facility would have been useful in Wotton Tramway days or under special circumstances. The siding leading from the Brill direction (bottom right-hand corner) was the one extended past the shaded station house at the Ashendon to Dorton road corner, and on to the embankment during construction of the 'Joint'.

Mike Crosbie

One of the telegraphic instruments used on the branch.

Bill George Collection

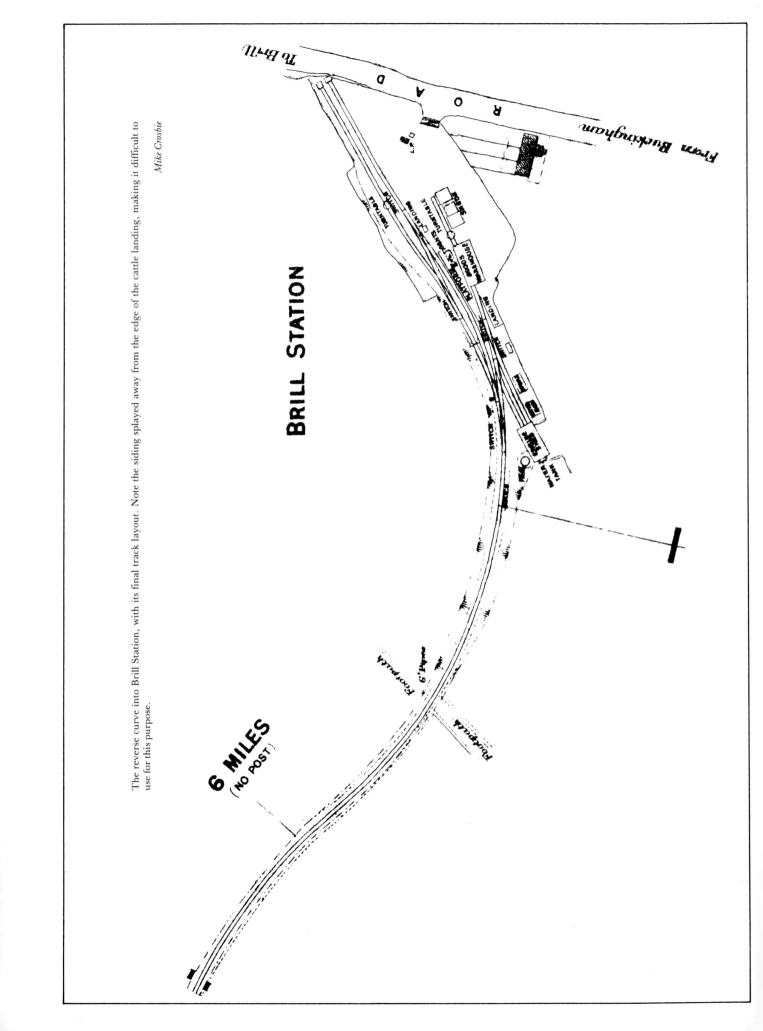

The reverse curve into Brill Station, with its final track layout. Note the siding splayed away from the edge of the cattle landing, making it difficult to use for this purpose.

Mike Crosbie

BRILL STATION

6 MILES
(NO POST)

Brill, a minor but neatly kept station in the 1920s. This study affords a good view of the cattle dock, which was put out of alignment with the track relaid in Metropolitan days. In the distance is Muswell Hill; a reminder of the obstacle that confronted the extension to Oxford.

L&GRP/Courtesy David & Charles

Surely one of the most modest and least imposing of station entrances at Brill. Nothing could be less assuming than a couple of six-bar gates. On the right is the weighbridge and hut, whilst on the left is the ale store. The platform was just behind this.

London Transport Executive

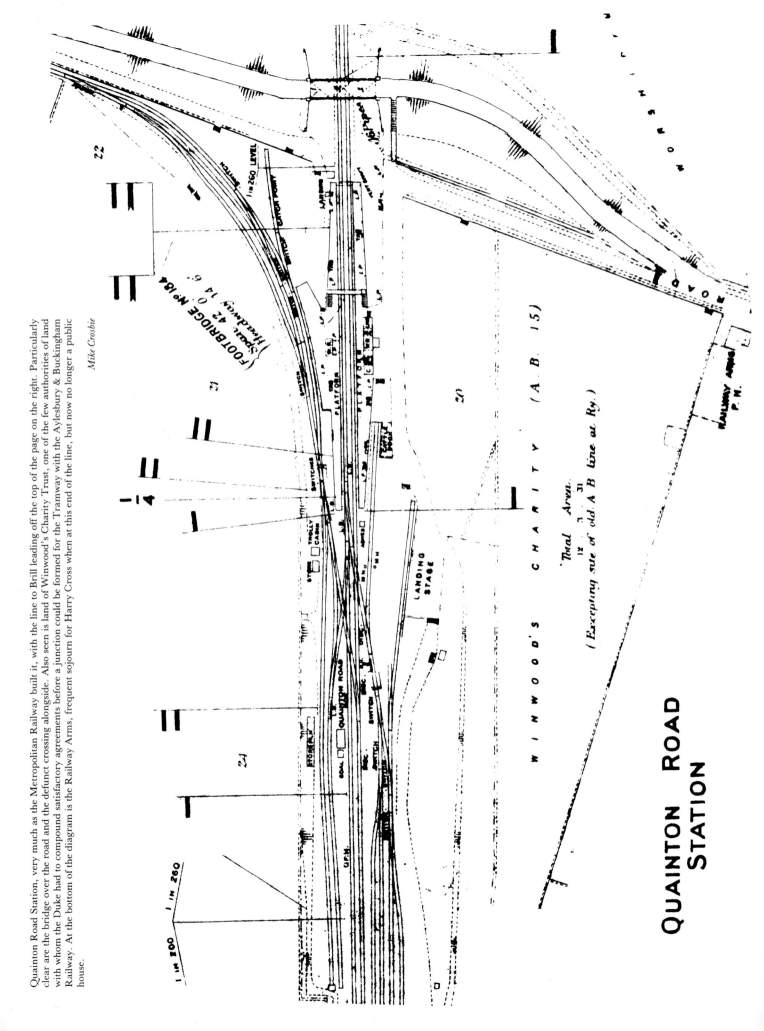

Quainton Road Station, very much as the Metropolitan Railway built it, with the line to Brill leading off the top of the page on the right. Particularly clear are the bridge over the road and the defunct crossing alongside. Also seen is land of Winwood's Charity Trust, one of the few authorities of land with whom the Duke had to compound satisfactory agreements before a junction could be formed for the Tramway with the Aylesbury & Buckingham Railway. At the bottom of the diagram is the Railway Arms, frequent sojourn for Harry Cross when at this end of the line, but now no longer a public house.

Mike Crosbie

QUAINTON ROAD STATION

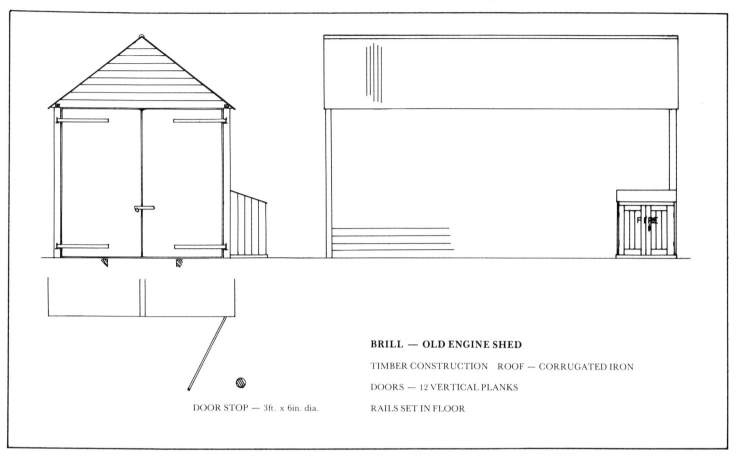

BRILL — OLD ENGINE SHED

TIMBER CONSTRUCTION   ROOF — CORRUGATED IRON

DOORS — 12 VERTICAL PLANKS

RAILS SET IN FLOOR

DOOR STOP — 3ft. x 6in. dia.

The first of the locomotive sheds at Brill that housed the Aveling Porter engines and the Bagnall locomotive, *Wotton*.

Mike Crosbie

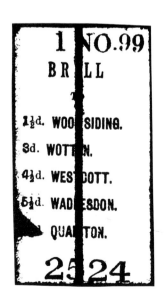

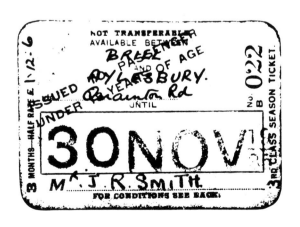

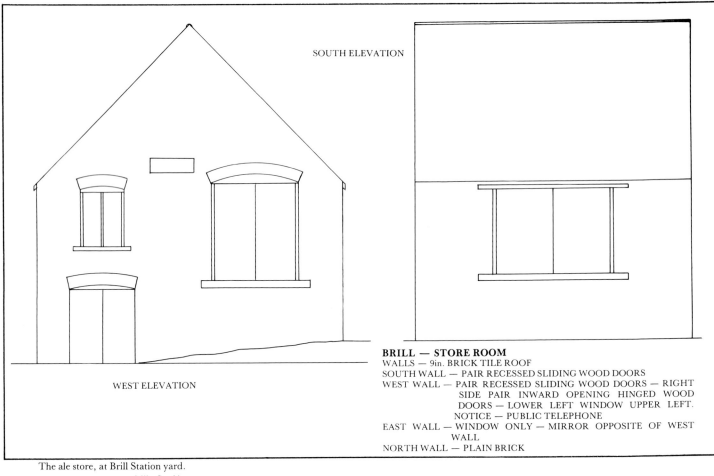

SOUTH ELEVATION

WEST ELEVATION

BRILL — STORE ROOM
WALLS — 9in. BRICK TILE ROOF
SOUTH WALL — PAIR RECESSED SLIDING WOOD DOORS
WEST WALL — PAIR RECESSED SLIDING WOOD DOORS — RIGHT
              SIDE PAIR INWARD OPENING HINGED WOOD
              DOORS — LOWER LEFT WINDOW UPPER LEFT.
              NOTICE — PUBLIC TELEPHONE
EAST WALL — WINDOW ONLY — MIRROR OPPOSITE OF WEST
              WALL
NORTH WALL — PLAIN BRICK

The ale store, at Brill Station yard.
Mike Crosbie

Both drawings on this page are in 4mm. to 1ft. scale.

Brill Station weighbridge hut, in 9in. brick with a corrugated-iron roof.
Mike Crosbie

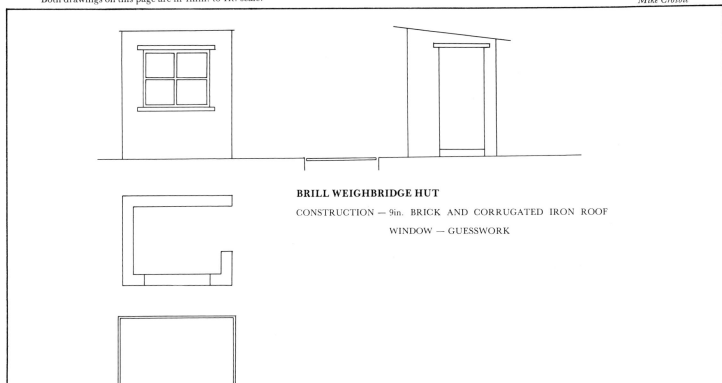

BRILL WEIGHBRIDGE HUT

CONSTRUCTION — 9in. BRICK AND CORRUGATED IRON ROOF

WINDOW — GUESSWORK

CHAPTER FOUR

The Brill Branch

Brill Station, the well-worn early platform in the foreground rising to the stout Metropolitan structure. The A class tank waits with its single brake composite in seeming isolation alongside the well-postered station building. The Metropolitan and LNER poster board lettering is a reminder of the 'Joint' interest, whilst the village name shines boldly and independently from the oil lamps. The building facing the train, with its doors open and far window visible, is the Brill Station locomotive shed.

London Transport Executive

On the first day of December 1899, the Tramway became, in effect, a branch of the Metropolitan Railway. It is a fact of historical serendipity that has provoked the curiosity of railway devotees ever since it happened. Within the concept of an arterial web of rails criss-crossing London, that there should be sleepy outposts like Westcott, Wotton and Wood Siding, seems to draw a comparison of very diverse scale. Nevertheless, the isolation of the Tramway was now at an end, and so too, to a degree, was its parsimonious condition.

The Metropolitan Railway Engineer did some slewing of the track at Quainton Road Station to allow the ease of moving their coaches on to the branch without fouling the platform face. This took place on 6th November 1899, after one coach had been slightly damaged in late October.

The use of larger engines on the line was restricted, as always, by the limited construction of the permanent way which, although rebuilt with transverse sleepering, was laid with light profile flat bottom rail. The Metropolitan Railway was, therefore, obliged to purchase the Manning Wardle locomotives to continue running the line. Not surprisingly, they were concerned to improve the service in keeping with the effort they had put into the rebuilding of the Aylesbury to Verney Line. The expanding prospect of what became termed 'Metroland' had yet to settle into its limits. Therefore, Brill and its environs could still be encompassed within this optimistic potential. Acceleration of the timetable was restricted by the governed speed of 12m.p.h., plus the frequent derailments. Engine No. 2 committed this graceless demeanor on 27th

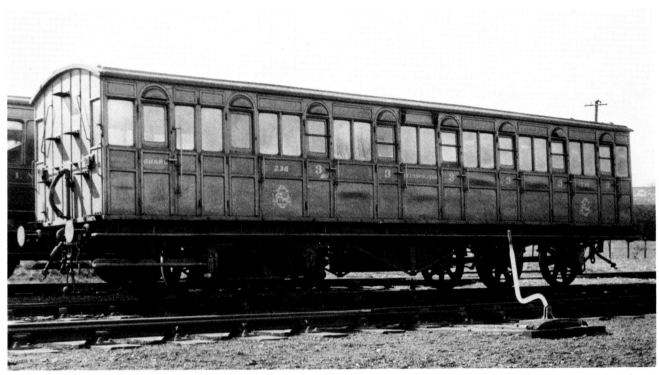

The vertical lines of one of the Oldbury stock of the Metropolitan, a brake third, sent to work the branch by that company. There is an antique flavour about the vehicles, reminiscent of early GWR 'Long Charleys'. Conversion to oil lamps would certainly enhance the period flavour.

L&GRP/Courtesy David & Charles

London Transport serves Brill and district as A class locomotive No. 23 leaves Quainton for that destination, with the modified Metropolitan coach and the new owner's name on the tank sides.

John Pritchett Collection

OXFORD AND AYLESBURY TRAMROAD SERVICE.

From BRILL. WEEK-DAYS. | SUNDAYS | To BRILL. WEEK-DAYS. | SUNDAYS.

TRAM STATIONS.		a.m.	a.m.	p.m.	p.m.	S O p.m.	a.m.	p.m.
Brill	dep.	8 40	10 32	3 10	5 30	7 23	7 0	5 35
Wood Siding*	„	*	*	*	*	*	*	*
Wotton	„	9 5	10 49	3 27	5 48	7 40	7 18	5 53
Westcott*	„	*	*	*	*	*	*	*
Waddesdon	„	9 22	11 1	3 39	6 1	7 52	7 30	6 6
Quainton Road	arr.	9 30	11 9	3 47	6 10	8 0	7 40	6 15

		a.m.	p.m.	p.m.	p.m.	p.m.		
Quainton Rd., dep. for Verney J.		9 40	11 57	4 3	6 39	8 3	...	·
Grandboro' Road	arr.	9 51	12 7	4 11	6 49	8 10	...	...
Winslow Road	„	9 56	12 13	4 15	6 53	8 14	...	...
Verney Junction		10 1	12 17	4 18	6 57	8 17	...	...

		a.m.	a.m.	p.m.	p.m.	p.m.	a.m.	p.m.
Quainton Rd., depart for Baker St.		9 44	11 13	3 49	6 19	8 6	7 53	6 24
Waddesdon Manor	arr.	9 50	11 15	3 53	6 23	8 10	7 57	6 28
Aylesbury	„	10 0	11 28	4 6	6 32	8 23	8 6	6 37
Baker Street	„	11 32	1 10	5 47	8 5	10 0	9 45	8 5

TRAM STATIONS.		a.m.	a.m.	p.m.	p.m.	p.m.	a.m.	p.m.
Baker Street	dep.	7 49	9 43	2 20	†4 55	6 21	9 5	3 30
Aylesbury	„	9 23	11 40	3 50	6 23	7 50	10 52	5 2
Waddesdon Manor	„	9 35	11 52	3 59	6 34	7 59	11 10	5 11
Quainton Road Station	arr.	9 39	11 56	4 3	6 39	8 3	11 16	5 15

		a.m.	a.m.	p.m.	p.m.	p.m.	a.m.	p.m.
Verney Junction	dep.	9 25	10 50	3 28	6 0	7 45	...	6 5
Winslow Road	„	9 30	10 55	3 33	6 4	7 50	...	6 10
Grandboro' Road	„	9 35	11 0	3 38	6 9	7 55	...	6 16
Quainton Road Station	arr.	9 42	11 10	3 48	6 17	8 5	...	6 23

TRAM STATIONS.		a.m.	p.m.	p.m.	p.m.	S O p.m.	a.m.	p.m.
Quainton Rd.Stn., depart for Brill		9 50	12 04	4 8	6 42	8 15	11 18	6 30
Waddesdon	dep.	9 59	12 9	4 16	6 50	8 23	11 26	6 38
Westcott*	„	*	*	*	*	*	*	*
Wotton	„	10 12	12 22	4 29	7 3	8 36	11 39	6 51
Wood Siding*	„	*	*	*	*	*	*	*
Brill	arr.	10 28	12 40	4 45	7 19	8 53	11 55	7 9

* Passengers wishing to alight at Westcott & Wood Siding Stations should inform the Guard at the previous Station, the train will also call at these Stations as required to take up passengers. † Change at Northwood.

FARES BETWEEN THE UNDERMENTIONED STATIONS.

	WADDESDON.				WESTCOTT.				WOTTON.				WOOD SIDING.				BRILL.			
	SINGLE.		RETURN.		SINGLE.		RETURN.		SINGLE.		RETURN.		SINGLE.		RETURN.		SINGLE.		RETURN.	
	1	3	1	3	1	3	1	3	1	3	1	3	1	3	1	3	1	3	1	3
	s. d.	s. d.	s. d.	s. d.	s. d.	s. d.	s. d.	s. d.	s. d.	s. d.	s. d.	s. d.	s. d.	s. d.	s. d.	s. d.	s. d.	s. d.	s. d.	s. d.
Brill	...	0 5½	...	0 8½	...	0 4½	...	0 7	...	0 3	...	0 4½	...	0 1½	...	0 2½	...	...	...	...
Wood Siding	...	0 4	...	0 6	...	0 3½	...	0 5	...	0 1½	...	0 2½	...	...	...	...	...	0 1½	...	0 2½
Wotton	...	0 2½	...	0 4	...	0 2	...	0 3	...	...	...	...	...	0 1½	...	0 2½	...	0 3	...	0 4½
Westcott	...	0 1	...	0 1½	...	...	...	...	...	0 2	...	0 3	...	0 3½	...	0 5	...	0 4½	...	0 7
Waddesdon	...	...	...	...	...	0 1	...	0 1½	...	0 2½	...	0 4	...	0 4	...	0 6	...	0 5½	...	0 8½
Quainton Road	...	0 1½	...	0 2½	...	0 2	...	0 3	...	0 4	...	0 6	...	0 5½	...	0 8½	...	0 7	...	0 9½
Verney Junction	1 1	0 7½	1 8	0 11½	1 2	0 8	1 9	1 0	1 4	0 10	2 0	1 3	1 6	0 11½	2 3	1 5½	1 8	1 0½	2 4	1 6½
Aylesbury	1 1	0 7½	1 8	0 11½	1 2	0 8	1 9	1 0	1 4	0 10	2 0	1 3	1 6	0 11½	2 3	1 5½	1 6	1 0½	2 4	1 6½
Baker Street	7 0	3 6½	10 6	5 4½	7 0	3 7	10 6	5 5	7 2	3 9	10 9	5 8	7 3	3 10½	11 0	5 10½	7 4	3 11½	11 0	5 11½

An extract from the Metropolitan Railway Guide of 1906, the Brill Branch service, including fares through to Baker Street. The timing was reasonable on the Brill branch for the Manning Wardle engines to make the connections at Quainton Road, providing of course that there were none of the familiar hold-ups to this rustic byway. The fare of 5¾d. (2½p) appeared for a short time on the Wotton Tramway in May 1898.

Mike Horne Collection

March 1903. Possibly in a pique of frustration, the shed foreman at Aylesbury sent one of the jaundiced D class engines to take over the service, No. 71, which damaged the trackwork at Brill and brought the matter of the permanent way to a head. The Metropolitan Railway bought six of these 2-4-0 D class engines from Sharp Stewart & Co. Ltd. in 1895 to replace some L&NWR engines loaned by them to work the Aylesbury to Verney Junction service. The class did not prove very successful on passenger work with a disturbing predilection to blowbacks; this brought about their almost exclusive allocation to goods work. Two of the class, Nos. 71 and 72, were kept at Aylesbury Shed, until the engines departed the service of the Metropolitan Railway along with their four sisters, between 1916 and 1922.

Returning to the situation at Brill, this had to be put right fairly quickly and, by 27th April, the station had been entirely relaid in bullhead rail. Subsequent parts of the remainder of the route were relaid back to Quainton throughout the summer of the same year and, by 10th August, the operation was complete. The rail used was track that had been displaced from other parts of the system that was still serviceable for branch line use. For the time being, the Manning Wardle locomotives still continued to work the service, according to Metropolitan drivers often in excess of the 12m.p.h. limit, which rather suggests that the governors were removed. They also became a

familiar sight at Aylesbury locomotive shed, as they would be kept there for boiler washouts and maintenance whilst the sister engine remained at Brill Shed. This was done on a weekly rota basis.

Although motive power was not, for the time being, changed, the better permanent way probably extended the stay of the Manning Wardle locomotives, and there was to be a marginal improvement in coaching stock. Jones had applied to John Bell of the Metropolitan Railway for better coaching facilities when the latter took over the running of the line. What eventually did transpire was a rather old third class carriage with seven compartments (70 seats) plus a guard's compartment. Before delivery to the branch it was converted from gas to oil heating. Any form of heating would have been a welcome improvement to tramway patrons, as it was the first vehicle to run on the line so equipped. It was delivered to the line on the morning of 4th October 1899. It was for this vehicle that the engineer had to slew the track at Quainton in the following month. With the introduction of this coach, the station platforms along the branch would be useless for proper embarking and alighting, being at rail height, therefore it was necessary for the Metropolitan Railway to build new platforms to a standard height of 36 inches and from 80 to 100ft. in length. Once more utilising defunct material, the company built them ingeniously from old railway sleepers on an earth base.

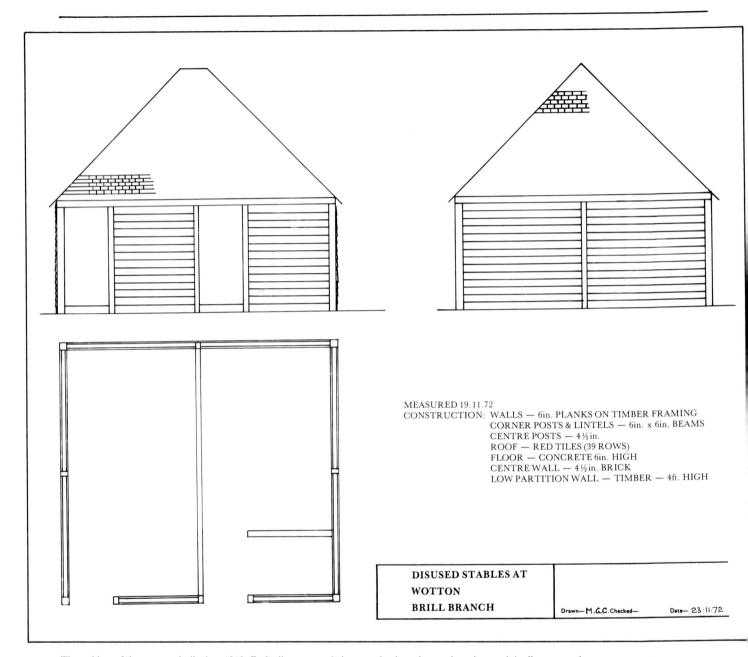

MEASURED 19.11.72
CONSTRUCTION: WALLS — 6in. PLANKS ON TIMBER FRAMING
                        CORNER POSTS & LINTELS — 6in. x 6in. BEAMS
                        CENTRE POSTS — 4½in.
                        ROOF — RED TILES (39 ROWS)
                        FLOOR — CONCRETE 6in. HIGH
                        CENTRE WALL — 4½in. BRICK
                        LOW PARTITION WALL — TIMBER — 4ft. HIGH

DISUSED STABLES AT
WOTTON
BRILL BRANCH   Drawn— M.G.C. Checked—   Date— 23·11·72

The stables at Wotton, as rebuilt circa 1910. Early diagrams and photographs show them to have been originally rectangular.

Mike Crosbie

As the Brill line now operated under the control of the Metropolitan & Great Central Joint Committee, correspondence to the Board of Trade to ask for an official inspection by them, in view of a desired speed increase on the line to 25m.p.h., carried the signature of one of the railway age's famous names, General Manager of the Great Central Railway, Sam Fay; this was on 1st November 1911. The inspecting officer on this occasion was Colonel von Donop, who mentioned that the 'new' bullhead rail was, in fact, displaced worn rail but was efficiently installed and he could see no reason why a speed of 25m.p.h. could not be acceded to from the previous 12m.p.h. He did, however, understandably, maintain the speeds of 8m.p.h. over crossings and 4m.p.h. at Thame Lodge. He also subjected his

approval to the installation of traps being put in at the west end of Quainton Station Yard and at the siding of Brill Station.

At about the same time, the Metropolitan Railway sent an inspecting engineer to report on the condition of rolling stock on the Tramway, who made the following conclusions. 'Two coaches, the Bristol Carriage & Wagon Co. vehicles, in need of slight repair and repainting and varnishing and altogether too light for the normal railway use'. He observed, disconcertingly, that they were apt to sway on the frames during the strain of haulage. To this, Jones suggested the remedy of a partition to strengthen the body. The inspecting officer, rather coldy, added that he thought two partitions would be needed! On the subject of the old Wotton Tramway composite vehicle, this had served

Waddesdon Station, looking from the Quainton end to the level crossing. The possible date is sometime during the 1920s when the station sign was fixed to the main building and not free standing on posts, as later. The billboard fixed to lavatory wall is of Great Central vintage, whilst the poster, although unreadable, carries the discernible LNER lozenge of the period. The station yard on the left holds but a single wagon on its siding which still ends in the earlier timber-built stop. Modellers should note the sheeted mound of hay alongside, and various rolls of canvas lying around ready for use.
Ken Benest Collection

The crossing gates at Waddesdon, with interesting features in the Brill line's unique collection of crossing gates. On the scale plan it can be appreciated that an extensive overlap had to be maintained in order that the gates would complete their function across the road.
Drawn by Mike Crosbie

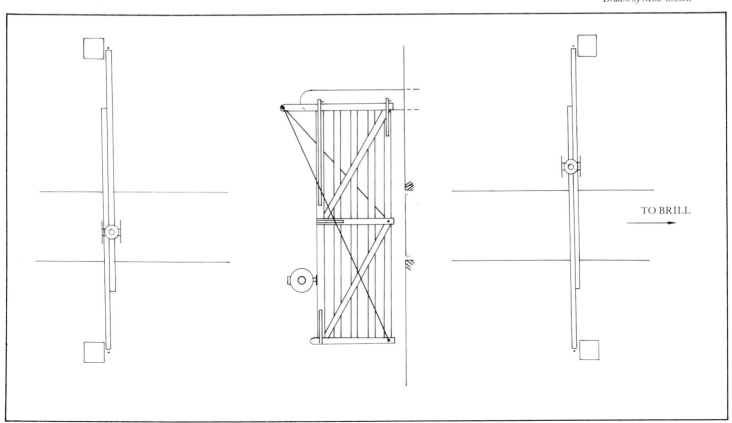

TO BRILL

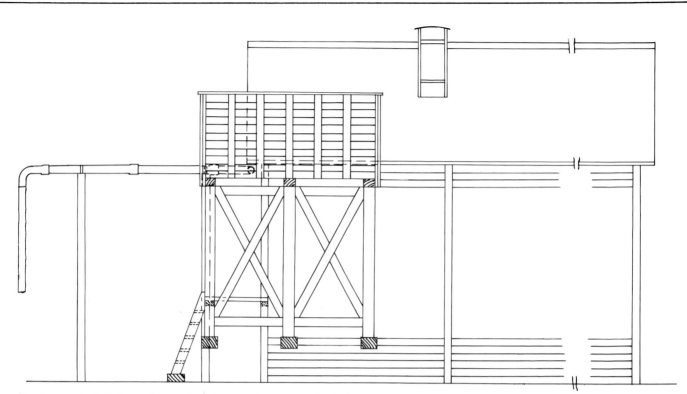

Structures on the Brill line tend to require rather more than average description, as they are unique in their lack of standardisation. The only structure to find any repetition at all is the design of the station buildings, and even in this case there is one exception — Westcott, which has vertical planking instead of horizontal. The basis for the lack of standardisation probably lies in the fact that, as an estate line, it drew on basic farming skills rather than specialised railway skills; this tended to give them a feral remoteness. The origin of most of them was probably little more than a basic rough sketch, and farming traditions did the rest. Such a structure is Brill locomotive shed, originally intended for carriage and wagon storage, with timber frame walls with a slate roof, and a zinc ventilating flue added later; a very basic building. The side elevation is a foreshortened view, but the plan view is entire, at the scale of 4mm. to 1ft. The water tank, with its contents drawn from a spring in Muswell Hill, is stoutly timbered, and was built alongside sometime early in the twentieth century. The arm of extended pipes is another example of specific adaption. The only illumination was from a single window in the back of the shed.

Drawn and researched by Mike Crosbie

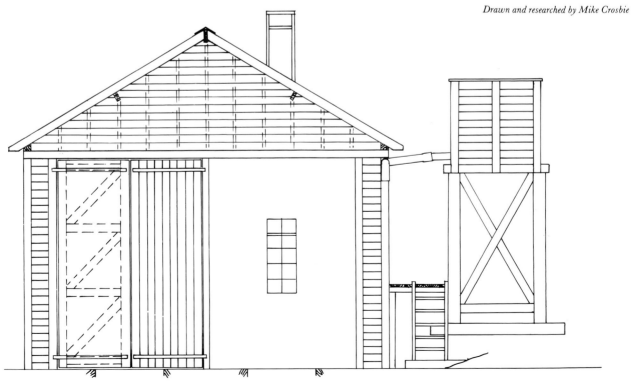

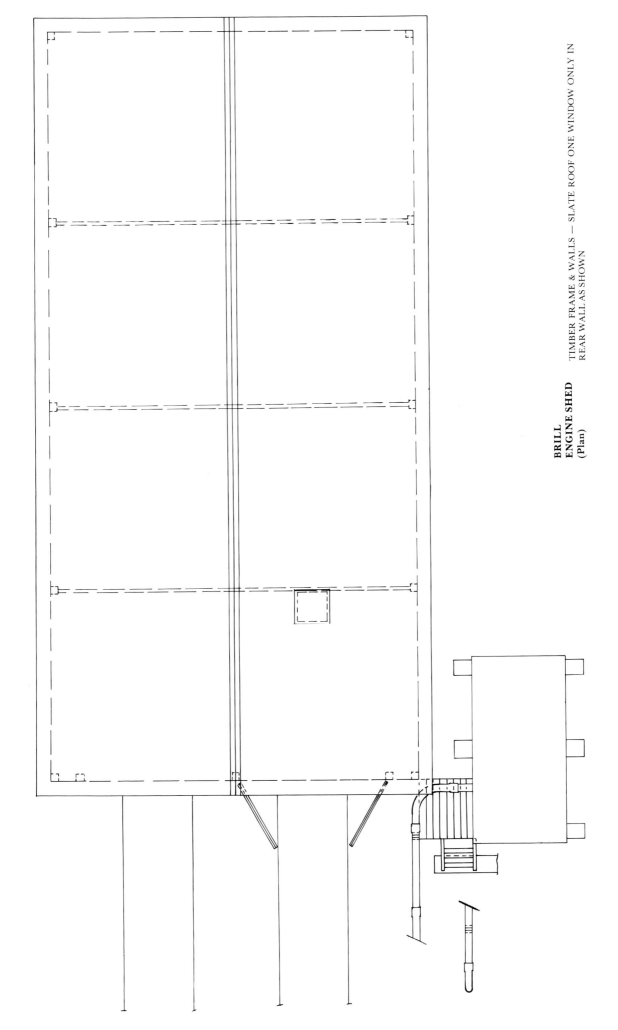

BRILL
ENGINE SHED
(Plan)

TIMBER FRAME & WALLS — SLATE ROOF ONE WINDOW ONLY IN
REAR WALL AS SHOWN

A photograph from the latter part of the nineteenth century, showing the crossroads at the foot of Brill Hill and the installation of Poore's Brickworks nearby, where so many bricks were made, taken along the road to the left to reach the building of Waddesdon Manor, via the Tramway. Note the hillside dug away behind the works which still remains as private dwellings. The windmill in the centre of the picture is not the one preserved at Brill at present; that is faintly visible at the right edge of the picture. The one in the centre was blown down, or collapsed, sometime during the 1920s. Brill originally had three windmills.

Buckinghamshire County Museum

for so long that it was well past its retirement day and was recommended to be removed from its wheels and be used as a platelayers' hut at Brill Station. This was indeed done, and there it lasted out its immobile days until the line's closure, thus surviving as the only piece of rolling stock to span the entire life of the line. The enigmatic old horse-drawn tramcar was described as having too short a wheelbase supporting a shabby interior, and too light in construction to be considered for use.

Although there were nine wagons, only one passed Railway Clearing House regulations, and all had dumb buffers.

The first Manning Wardle locomotive, *Huddersfield*, required rebuilding, which was tantamount to saying it needed scrapping, as it was valued at £150. The second Manning Wardle engine, once called *Earl Temple* but now renamed *Brill No. 1*, was considered to be in good condition but to have depreciated by some 33 per cent. The third Manning Wardle locomotive, and the pride of the fleet, *Wotton No. 2*, was given a clean bill of health — first class condition. A sum of £2,375, was paid by the Metropolitan Railway to Earl Temple for the latter two locomotives, two bogie cars and wagon No. 9. The slender resources of the Tramroad company are reflected by a further payment of £700 for its rolling stock, stores, tools and wagon No. 3, which was a low-sided truck used by the Tramway for carrying milk churns. This was considered to be worth a £6 repair but the two Bristol vehicles and the old tramcar were advertised for sale during the summer of 1900. The Bristol vehicles were sold to the Llanelly & Mynydd Mawr Railway and were transferred to Metropolitan bogies to reach their destination. Unfortunately, no account of the fate of the old horse-drawn tramcar has ever been discovered.

From now on, passenger rolling stock on the line would be drawn from a fleet of five rigid eight wheel coaches, one of which was previously mentioned, built by the Oldbury Carriage Company between 1865 and 1866. As these vehicles were rebodied about 1896, they came to the Tramway in a renovated condition.

By mid-1910, the Metropolitan Railway could at last shake off some of the torpor of a bucolic Tramway. With the track relaid and a Board of Trade inspection, speeds could be accelerated to a positive tour de force of 25m.p.h., which allowed a journey time between Quainton and Brill of about 35 minutes. The Manning Wardle engines were put up for sale in the hope of more appropriate use as contractors' engines. The oldest engine, *Huddersfield* had been sold in 1901 whilst the other two left the line about 1911. The era of the Brill branch was now drawn into the ambiance of the Metropolitan, with teak coaches assorted with open trucks, and the handsome A class tank at the head, the Metropolitan's oldest engines now released from the smokey labyrinths of subterranean London to work in semi-retirement in the fresh air of the Buckinghamshire countryside. Later, for a short time, they were lettered with the words 'London Transport' on their tank sides, which heightened their curio appearance as they steamed gently across country roads between hand-opened white gates.

Before the line achieved its modest elevation in status, with the departure of the Manning Wardle locomotives, there would be a loss much more personal, that of Ralph Augustus Jones who died on 14th April 1909. When the Metropolitan Railway took over running of the line, Jones had been retained as Manager on a salary of £300 per annum but, in February 1903, he was forced to retire owing to poor health. He did continue as Secretary to the O&AT until 7th August of the same year, when he finally retired on a pension of £75 per annum.

Arriving at Waddesden Road, A class No. 41 is seen with a train for Brill. It is still carrying the rope on the buffer beam for shunting the various sidings along the line, particularly Church Siding.

Roy Slaymaker Collection

BRILL BRANCH SERVICE.

WEEKDAYS.

TO BRILL.

	a.m.	a.m.	p.m.	p.m.	80 p.m.
BAKER STREET........dep.	7 56	11 0	2 19	4a10	7 20
AYLESBURY .... ,,	9 22	12 38	3 43	6a10	9 0
Verney Junction........ ,,	8 50	10 45	3 30	6 5	7 8
Quainton Road .... ,,	9 46	12 55	4 4	6 30	9 20
Waddesdon Road .... ,,	9 56	1 5	4 14	6 40	9 30
Westcott † .... ,,	†	†	†	†	†
Wotton .... ,,	10 9	1 18	4 27	6 53	9 43
Wood Siding † .... ,,	†	†	†	†	†
BRILL.................arr.	10 18	1 27	4 36	7 2	9 52

a—A Fast train leaves Marylebone at 5.0 p.m., Aylesbury arrive 5.46 p.m. and connects with 6 10 p.m. to Verney Junction

FROM BRILL.

	a.m.	a.m.	p.m.	p.m.	80 p.m.
BRILL.................dep.	7 57	10 30	3 7	5 40	8 37
Wood Siding † .... ,,	†	†	†	†	†
Wotton .... ,,	8 11	10 42	3 19	5 52	8 49
Westcott † .... ,,	†	†	†	†	†
Waddesdon Road .... ,,	8 27	10 56	3 33	6 6	9 3
Quainton Road ....arr.	8 33	11 2	3 39	6 12	9 9
Verney Junction........ ,,	10 21	12 16	4 15	6 45	—
AYLESBURY .... ,,	8 55	11 21	4 2	6 39	9 51
BAKER STREET........ ,,	10 25	1 13	5 42	8 6	11 18

Jones, in fact, survived Earl Temple, who died at Stowe in 1902, aged 55, by seven years. Upon his death his eldest son became Earl Temple, inheritor of the estate and the position of Chairman to the Oxford & Aylesbury Tramway, which was now a matter of little more than protocol. With the retirement of Jones, the Metropolitan Railway issued regulations for working the line. They also appointed one of their own men as secretary of the O&AT, a Mr Frank Huskins.

In the years between Jones' retirement and his death, it was possible for him to witness the most intensive period of railway development in the area. As the O&AT struggled to find a way to reach Oxford, the Manchester, Sheffield & Lincolnshire Railway projected their endeavour under the original stimulus of Edward Watkin; the extension to London. This prong southward against the run of former main line railways was planned to meet the new northward extension of the Metropolitan Railway at Quainton Road. It did, however, bring about a sequence of events that would regard the Tramway unfavourably, as a result of a somewhat thorny alliance between the two large companies which forced the northern company to seek an alternative route into the capital.

In this view of Westcott, looking towards Brill, one can clearly see the strong sleeper-built construction of the high platforms built by the Metropolitan Railway.

London Transport Executive

A view across the fields from Westcott platform towards Waddesdon. This provides a very good example of Brill line countryside, mostly flat arable or grazing land relieved by the arboreal stature of the magnificent oak or elm. The daughters of Wescott stationmaster Mr Joe Varney, (Miss Grace Varney and Miss Bernice Varney) can be seen crossing the line.

London Transport Executive

The Brill branch, eminently Metropolitan in an age when trains, sidings and marshalling yards were appellations of lettered names and colour styles from the thousands of private owner wagons in circulation. This mixed train of coal and passengers, about to leave for Brill, is probably one of the most favoured recollections of this unusual line. Note the dirt cover on the slidebars of the locomotive.

London Transport Executive

(Right):

As mentioned in the view of Wotton in the earlier photographs by Newton, the environs of the station were thickly wooded to the point of concealment. As is evident on this print of thirty years later, little has changed to spoil the perfect setting of a country railway. Even the bridge of the GW & GC Joint has mellowed into the pastorale; an open wagon on the goods siding, having brought, or is taking away the prefabricated sections of a wooden hut, with a man waiting with a few sacks, and the bicycle leaning against the door. Even the company posters appear a little self-consciously out of place. Nevertheless, the accelerating forces of change would soon catch up with Wotton, for within twelve months of this photograph all was gone for ever. Our gratitude to the camera is measureless in terms of a record of how it appeared. Of particular interest are the differing styles of oil lamps, the larger box shape near the office doorway, and a fascinating curved top style on the post in the foreground. Quite a number of this type appeared on the branch with the station name set high up on the facing glass. One regular user of the Tramway early this century, spoke of a special candle lamp in use at the stations then. As Wotton was the only station on a curve on the Tramway, it typifies the nature of sharp curves on the line as the rails curve out of view from both ends of the platform after a very short distance.

London Transport Executive

Bunker first working for No. 41 on this trip to Brill. The man on the platform is believed to be the late Aubrey Ewers, who spent a long period of his railway career working at various stations on the Aylesbury to Verney Junction and Brill line.

London Transport Executive

In the brilliance of summer sunshine, and the fullness of its wooded enclave, the station at Wood Siding can be said to identify strongly with its name. With No. 23 in London Transport livery, it probably typifies the eccentric association of this remote outpost to that mighty corporate transport system. As the fireman opens the gates, worthy of mention is the timber stop on the siding, which doubled as a milk landing for the main line.

H. C. Casserley

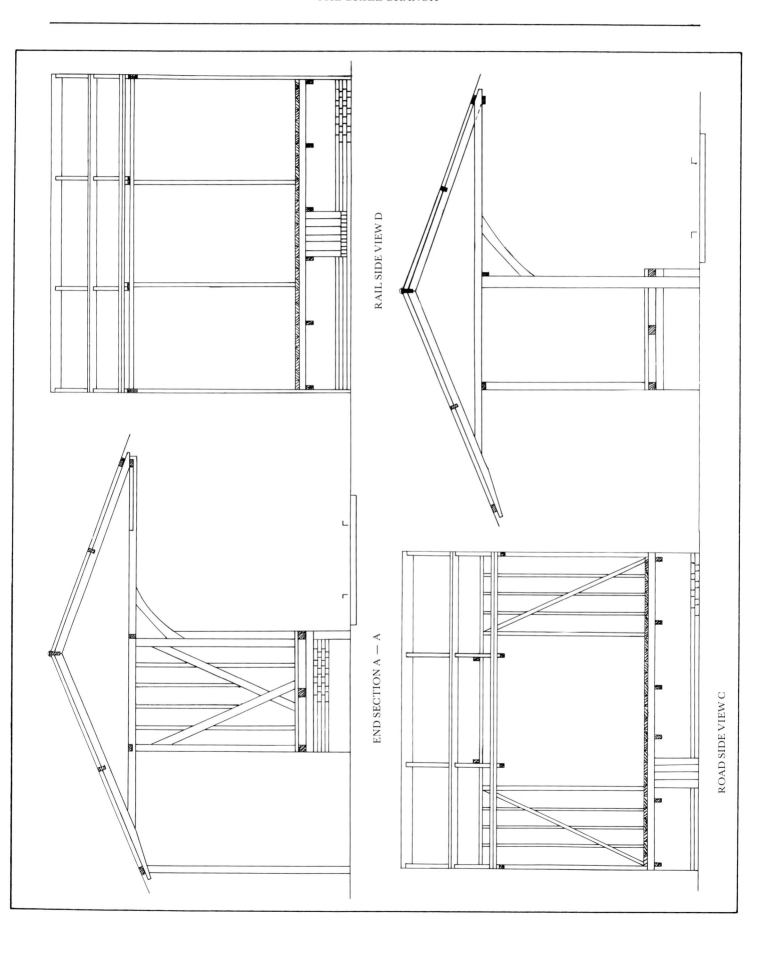

RAIL SIDE VIEW D

END SECTION A — A

ROAD SIDE VIEW C

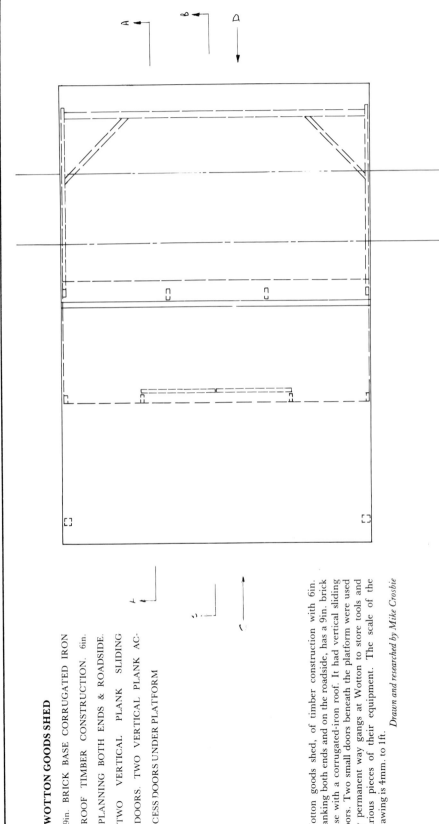

WOTTON GOODS SHED

9in. BRICK BASE CORRUGATED IRON
ROOF TIMBER CONSTRUCTION. 6in.
PLANKING BOTH ENDS & ROADSIDE.
TWO VERTICAL PLANK SLIDING
DOORS. TWO VERTICAL PLANK AC-
CESS DOORS UNDER PLATFORM

Wotton goods shed, of timber construction with 6in.
planking both ends and on the roadside, has a 9in. brick
base with a corrugated-iron roof. It had vertical sliding
doors. Two small doors beneath the platform were used
by permanent way gangs at Wotton to store tools and
various pieces of their equipment. The scale of the
drawing is 4mm. to 1ft.

Drawn and researched by Mike Crosbie

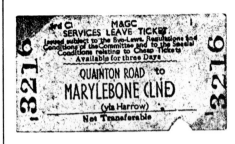

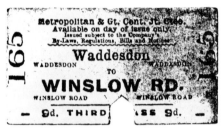

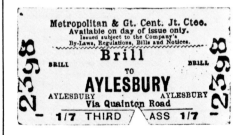

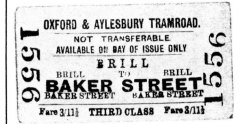

The latter day Wood Siding, looking from the Brill end.

Roy Slaymaker Collection

No. 23 crossing Kingswood Lane at Wood Siding, on the way to Brill.

H. C. Casserley

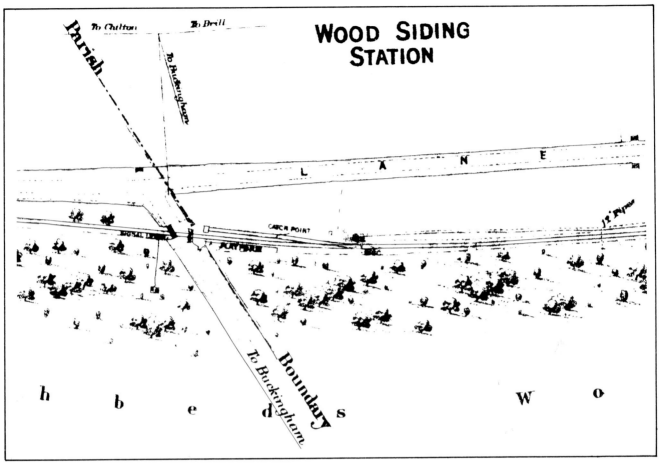

A ground plan of Wood Siding, circa 1910. Note the signal switch immediately to the Quainton side of the crossing gates. This was for a signal post just under a quarter of a mile away on the curve from Thame Lodge.

Mike Crosbie Collection

After the northern company had adopted the new name of the Great Central Railway, connection was made at Quainton early in 1898. The Metropolitan Railway had not laid their seal to this agreement, as General Managers of both companies, W. Pollit (GCR) and J. Bell (Metropolitan), were old adversaries and inevitable friction occurred, which brought about a great deal of rancour and disagreement, forcing the GCR to contemplate alternatives, even at some expense. What eventually transpired were two agreements with the GWR for link lines; one from Woodford Halse to Banbury and another linking up with the GWR's proposed shorter route to Birmingham from Princes Risborough via Aynho, connecting with the 1850 roundabout way through Oxford — a cut-off line, in fact. In the amity of mutual interest, a GWR & GCR Joint Committee was formed for the building of part of this line on 1st August 1899, six months after the GCR passenger service was already operating on their new main line. Although the GWR alternative route was from Old Oak Common through Ashendon to Aynho, forming a junction with the old route there, the GCR were only to make use of the line from their Marylebone terminus to a junction at Northolt, up the line as far as Ashendon where they built another flying junction for their alternative line cross-country to Grendon Underwood, and back to their main line metals. This short line affected the Tramway as it cut directly across its path at Wotton and eventually caused another

station there. Construction for the new line from London began in 1901 whilst the Ashendon to Grendon Underwood line was started in 1902.

At Wotton, the line was built above the Tramway, with an embankment and plate girder bridge for the easement of which the GWR and GCR Joint Committee paid the O&AT £100. The irony of its arrival was heightened by the fact that the Tramway contributed to the development of the interloper by bringing much of the material to the site. Along with trains of brick, timber and steel, came also the men and their horses together with prefabricated wooden huts which they set up as a small community in the vicinity of the station, along with their families. A more orderly process of temporary industrial colonisation was now altruistically forced upon the railway's building contractors. A far cry from the period of rumbustious hard drinking rough men, living in earth huts and irreligious squalor. Notwithstanding, for a time, the sleepy homesteads of Wotton reverberated to the sounds of heavy construction, with steam locomotives, cranes and horses straining with wagons of spoil, or timber felled on the estate. As the gashed wealds of earth receded to an embankment across the site, Wotton Tramway Station itself bustled with activity, and amongst the scattering of huts and workshops was a timber locomotive shed. One of the sidings — the one that springs from the curve at the Brill end of the station — was extended for quite a distance to

A view approaching Wood Siding crossing gates from the Quainton direction. A thread of rails through the ancient wood, the limits implied rather than enforced with post and wire fencing.

London Transport Executive

Brill Brickworks, seen from the hill, rather than from the railway side. The clay was conveyed from the hill to the tall building in the centre, in front of the chimney, where it was dried and broken down to a crumbly texture before being pressed into shape. The view from this angle shows that the works had three chimneys. Although overgrown, the set of narrow gauge rails are visible. These held the trucks that carried the freshly dug clay to the timber trestle conveyors on the right. Behind the works is the thickly wooded land enclosing the Tramway.

Buckinghamshire County Museum

Metropolitan tank No. 41 waits at Brill Station with its familiar assembly of two coal wagons and a brake composite coach. The coal merchants are Stevco (Stevens Coal Merchants of Oxford). This merchant is still in business in that city. The second wagon is even more local, being that of Thomas Green of Brill.

London Transport Executive

A reflective moment for the staff of Brill Station, as No. 23 waits with its single coach to return to Quainton. A conversation, possibly about the future of the line, is taking place between Fireman Bill Newton and George Porter. The man looking on with a parcel in his hand is Charles Pullen, one of three postmen at Brill. The date of the scene is 8th April 1933.

H. C. Casserley

reach along the newly developing permanent way. This was used by three M type Manning Wardle locomotives which the contractor brought to work upon the line. The three locomotives were called *Peterhead, Lliedi,* and *Haddenham.*

The new line opened in November 1905, and although it had been constructed as part of an agreement with the GWR, it was, in concept and working, a GCR undertaking, and an alternative to the use of the Metropolitan line.

The remainder of the GWR route to Aynho from Ashendon Junction was not opened until 1910. This too was to affect the Tramway, but to a lesser degree. At Wotton, the Tramway had sorely felt the incursion upon its preserve of thirty three years, with an extensive and commodious new station overshadowing it, giving direct access both north and south. Bearing the rub still further, another station was opened where the new line crossed the Roman Akeman Street, the original ancient route between St. Albans and Bath, connecting, locally, Bicester and Aylesbury. The station was planned with the firm intention of drawing on the local agricultural traffic, as the farming community was directly consulted on the need and the siting of it. The farmers mentioned that they were particularly keen on the transit of large consignments of livestock for fattening and sheep.

As mentioned, the new GWR line north to Birmingham, via Aynho and Banbury, brought turmoil to another part of the Tramway, at the rustic spot of Wood Siding. The survey for this line cut, with hairs breadth precision, beneath the site of Wood Siding Station, which required a plate girder bridge to carry the line of the Tramway above it. When this was completed, there was some acrimony between the representatives

for Earl Temple and the Metropolitan Railway, as the latter had allowed the work to proceed without consulting the Earl, and exacted some few hundred pounds in compensation for the same. In the end, the certain loser was the Tramway, with its lapsed powers to extend to Oxford unfulfilled and the steady build-up of competition for all the traffic that it drew upon. With the opening of the new GWR route in April 1910, the village of Brill was to have its name appear on a rival station nameboard. Although much further away from the village than even the Tramway, and closer by far to the village of Ludgershall, the new station of Brill & Ludgershall would still receive competitive interest from the farming community and coal merchants. This was indeed the final manifestation of railway development in the area which had, in fifteen years, witnessed a bewildering surge of railway interest, from the prosaic Aylesbury & Buckingham Railway, with a little Tramway arm tacked on, to the prospect of London commuter expansion and other railways criss-crossing the area and keen to serve it, whilst the Tramway remained meshed in between.

The expensive gambit of the GCR alternative route did, in fact, temporise the Metropolitan's attitude, and an Act forming the Metropolitan & Great Central Joint Committee became effective on 2nd April 1906, but it was not until 11th June 1913 that the final seal was put on working arrangements between the two companies. This was to administer all lines from Harrow South Junction to Verney Junction, plus the running rights on the Chesham branch and the Brill branch. In effect, the GCR had now portioned an interest in the Tramway.

Reconciliations and the zenith of railway accessibility must be seen as a poignant contrast in the year 1914, for with the

On 21st May 1934, No. 41 has just completed another journey of the seemingly eternal Tramway, which had, in fact, less than two years of life left.

H. F. Wheeler

outbreak of World War I, and the mighty behemoth of carnage rising out of the Flanders mud, even the Brill line could not be totally removed from its reality; for this harbinger of dreadful change wrought every corner of the land.

The war brought a striking contrast in the form of two locomotive exhausts echoing the woods and fields, with five full passenger coaches between them. It must have made quite a sight on this line, as they wound their slow progress alongside the roads, across the fields and positively serpentine over the road crossings, whose gates had never been held open so long before. This prodigal engine power came at last to rest, like the excursionist train of so long ago, at the sleepy outpost of Wood Siding. By strong contrast with that train, however, this was a troop train. In retrospect, few things could have been more stirringly tragic in 1914 than a train full of young Army cadets alighting at this spot. Wotton House had been made available to the armed forces, and a camp had been set up in the grounds for the soldiery in a field adjoining the Ludgershall to Kingswood Road. Training was to be undertaken around the area, including Brill. The house itself was organised as offices and a billet for Army staff.

Relieved of their passengers the two A class tanks and their trains went to Brill Station, where the front engine was uncoupled and ran on to the loop, enabling the rear engine to push the train forward towards the stops. The other engine then moved off the loop and in front of the train whereupon it was coupled with the second engine, and in this form they returned to Quainton.

As mentioned earlier, the war accelerated the decline of Westcott Gasworks, which finally closed in 1916, with the resulting loss of this sorely needed traffic. The works was not demolished until 1918, coincidentally, not by the cause of the war but the expiration of the lease. On 31st December 1915, the Kingswood line closed. The rails did remain edging a grassy pathway until circa 1918 when two estate workers went along with a sledge hammer and cutting tool and simply knocked off the flange bolts. The rails were then loaded on to horse-drawn carts and taken for scrap. The branch was cut back as far as the coal wharf at Church Siding which served the needs of Wotton House.

As a result of the development of huge brick-making plants like the one at Calvert, Brill Brickworks ceased production and closed down in 1911. It was demolished shortly afterwards. Fortunately, the siding traffic was not lost to the Tramway but changed its form. This was the result of an enterprising local farmer named W. E. Fenemore who had invented and organised the production of his patent hay-loading machine. He started to produce the machines at his farm near Wotton, called Moat Farm, but when the brickworks site became abandoned, he considered it ideal for the expansion of his business, having a rail siding. This was good news for the Tramway who could ill afford to lose any customer and needed every new one it could find. The hay-loader works required a great deal of timber, iron and fuel to produce its hundred machines a year, which

Steamily, No. 41 replenishes her tanks at the individually-styled Brill Shed water tank on 15th March 1930. A wagon of Thomas Green, coal merchant, Brill, is obviously being shunted. Note the Annett's patent locking box on the point lever on the right. This photograph illustrates, clearly, the reason for this type of engine having such a narrow cab. Originally cabless, when this was added it was necessary to exclude the tank fillers that were situated close to the cab area.

H. C. Casserley

Fenemore hoped to improve upon. Luckily for Brill and district, the new business was able to employ people made redundant by the closing down of the brickworks.

After the first year on the site, he doubled his original production figure of one hundred machines a year along with the manufacture of hay-holders. The latter was a cart or wain that carried the hay and, with each machine, there was usually a requirement of three; one collecting the hay in the field, one journeying between this and the hay-loader, with another working with the machine. Good movement would require a rotation of the three. The best year on the site was 1920 when the company produced something in the region of 256 hay-loaders. As the company also did a lot of farm repair and farrier work, as well as general timber construction work, it provided a welcome replacement to the business lost with the closure of the brickworks. Coal, steel and timber in enormous 60ft. baulks were brought down the line and shunted over the road along the siding and into the works, whilst machines coming out were bound for diverse places as far away as Australia and New Zealand.

During the 1920s, Massey Harris brought out their version of a hay-loader in large scale mass production which, like the brick-making business before, began to undercut the smaller manufacturer. As the demand for Fenemore machines began to decrease, competition to the Tramway began to increase. It was found to be more convenient, in some cases, to take machines to the Wotton Station of the GWR & GCR Joint, and the Brill & Ludgershall Station of the GWR rather than on the Tramway.

However, there was still a considerable timber business and this was helped enormously, in 1928, with the installation of electricity for the powerful wood saws. A multiplicity of products were turned out from the site, including thousands of coffin boards.

A potent thought for the year 1920 was the legacy of war, for in that year, 101,000 motor goods vehicles had been registered in Britain. It was the beginning of an impetus that would carry a new transport revolution. The railway high water mark had been reached in 1914; from now on it was in a running battle against road expansion, with short feeder lines like the Tramway vulnerably exposed to its first effects. Quietly the Brill branch Sunday service was discontinued in 1920 and, on 1st October 1922, Waddesdon Manor Station became Waddesdon, whilst the Tramway station became Waddesdon Road.

In 1923, the Amalgamation of Railways Act of 1921 became effective and the four main groups of railways comprising the multiplicity of large and small railways came into being. A new name on the Brill Station signs was that of the London & North Eastern Railway which took over all former GCR interests including those of the Joint Committees, with the Metropolitan and GWR, which meant, in fact, that the two stations at Wotton were still partly under the same control. This brought about the need for only one stationmaster for both of them. What was left of the Tramway's singular identity was eroding at an accelerating rate.

In October 1929, the Oxford & Aylesbury Tramroad Company began negotiations with the Electric Railway Finance Company to sell all their assets. They knew full well that the writing was beginning to appear on the wall and, unfortunately for them, so did the Finance Company, who would doubtless find it difficult to see ground for investment. A valuation survey fixed a price of £24,050 around which negotiations haggled for over a year, but in the end came to nothing. They were unsuccessfully wound up on 5th January 1930.

In 1924, a year after the formation of the big four companies, the total national goods tonnage by rail was assessed as 80.8 million. Eleven years later, in 1935, the year that proved to be the last in the Tramway's life, goods for rail were assessed at 65.5 million tons, a drastic drop in just over a decade. By now there were 435,000 goods vehicle registered in Britain.

The 1923 amalgamation did not include the Metropolitan and District lines of London which, along with the road passenger services of the capital, were apportioned to a separate identity.

On 1st July 1933, the Metropolitan Railway became part of the newly-formed London Passenger Transport Board who, in turn, initiated a massive new works programme. This gave the immediate impression that London Transport reached out to Brill; beguilingly it was advertised as being on the underground system. It was not, however, good news for the line, which still suffered from its old problem of derailments causing disconcertingly abbreviated passenger journeys, which could provide little incentive for people to use the line. Indeed, loss of reliability is a virtual death sentence to any railway. Perhaps some of the fault may have lain with the original engineering of the line which, as laid down by the Duke, had not been intended for passenger use originally and thus was inherently at fault. A number of trains began to run totally empty of passengers whilst goods traffic, mainly coal, was consistent but slender. An example of this traffic in the early 1930s was supplied by Stevco Limited (Stevens Coal) of Oxford who supplied George Green, coal merchant of Brill. They supplied, as Wholesale Coal Factors, about three wagon loads a month, between 25 to 30 tons. The high spot of the year was the summer stocking order for Wotton House; this was about 100 tons. The coal came from Warwickshire; the Wotton order, always from Baddesley Colliery. The railway rate was about eight shillings (40p) per ton and wagon hire was one shilling per ton (5p).

Goods working was not a cause célèbre of the new London Transport, who would probably be more than happy to see the LNER absorb the local interests in that form. The large tank engines of the Metropolitan Railway had been sold to the LNER for that purpose. All things being considered, the fact that London Transport were looking toward extended electrification no further north than Amersham, leaving the former A&BR line and the Brill line to the devices of the LNER, who ran the main line service from Marylebone to the north, it is not difficult to imagine that the Oxford & Aylesbury Tramroad Company would be expecting some kind of correspondence from London Transport with regard to the Brill service. This arrived on 1st June 1935, and simply informed them that the LPTB wished to terminate its tenancy under the terms of the Bell letter.

In order to fulfil the rites of closure of their service, London Transport ran an inspection special along the line on 23rd July 1935. Having left Baker Street a few minutes after 1p.m., Brill Station was reached by 2.30p.m. Inspection of the line was performed with almost indecent haste, especially for this line, leaving Brill at 2.45p.m., and arriving back at Quainton shortly after 3p.m.

In view of the fact that the branch was trying to survive on fewer than fifty passenger journey bookings per day, with goods and minerals at approximately twenty tons per day, which amounted to the sum total of an annual loss of £4,000, closure could not have been much of a surprise to anyone.

The final membership of the O&AT Board consisted of only three; Earl Temple, who did not live at Wotton, held the post of Chairman, whilst his agent, Robert White, was a Director, along with W. E. Fenemore. To these gentlemen the departure of the lessees of the line could only find one conclusion.

With the expiration of the Metropolitan & GC Joint terms, set for 1st December 1935, the final train was scheduled to run on 30th November 1935, preceded by the ritual announcements of closure that became harrowingly familiar thirty years later.

One Charles E. Lee decided to take advantage of the diminishing time left to ride on the Brill tram, and published his eyewitness account in the *Railway Magazine* of October 1935. 'All of the line is laid with bullhead rails in chairs, but remains of the original bridge rails and flat bottom rails may be found in the sheds at Brill. There is no signalling, only one engine in steam and the driver carries the token key which unlocks the siding points. Level crossing gates, normally closed across the rails and locked, are opened by the guard or fireman, except at Westcott and Wotton stations where permanent staff is employed. At Wotton, the stationmaster of the adjacent LNER station is responsible also for the Brill line'.

With what became a familiar irony, the last train was packed, whilst at the stations and along the lineside there was a veritable furore of spectators assembled in the November rain. It could be approximated with reasonable certainty that this day, even with its bad weather, was probably the most populous in the entire history of the line. The A class engine, running bunker first, ran with her full complement of two coaches as she left Quainton, in the late evening. At Brill, there was quite a large assembly of villagers and people from many miles around who had come to pay their last respects. A chorus of 'Auld Lang Syne' strained through the black night of extinguishing oil lamps that were placed on the train, along with other station moveables, documents and staff. The same final tidying up was carried out at the other stations as the train went along leaving them sad and empty. There was a final ignominy for the train as fleets of motor cars pursued it on to the end. At 11.45p.m., it rounded the curve into Quainton, proudly carrying herself smokebox first and alighting its load of acolytes amongst the bemused staff. There was a ritual cutting of the rails on the stroke of midnight.

After the lapse of a few months, on 2nd April 1936, a party of interested purchasers and sightseers visited the now deserted Tramway stations. The sale of Tramway articles was carried out at each point by Messrs Burrows & Bradfield of Thame, under auction, and realised the grand total of £72 7s. 0d. (£72.35p) with four lots remaining unsold. The station houses were sold separately.

After a Board Meeting, on 5th January 1937, the O&AT petitioned to wind-up the concern in the High Court on 24th March of the same year. A Mr W. E. Fisher was appointed liquidator. He had completed his task by 1940. Had the line lasted longer than 1935, and continued until the outbreak of World War II, it would, as it later appeared, have brought about a compensatory situation at Westcott, as the line would have had to have a section removed for the building of the airfield there. Doubtless, under the emergency, there would have been little resistance from the Tramway to prevent this necessity, which would have probably meant closure anyway.

Eventually, all of the rails were removed for scrap by Ward, Scrap Metal Company of London, for £7,000, with the exception of those at Quainton Road which remained there as part of the sidings. As a revenue-earning railway preservation society still uses that part of the line, it could be stated, technically, that this hugely-foreshortened line is still earning money.

As for the local population's transport needs, the City of Oxford Motor Services introduced a bus service between Brill and Aylesbury calling at Wood Siding, Wotton Station, Westcott and Waddesdon, with departures from Brill at 1p.m. and 5.10p.m. and from Aylesbury at 3.30p.m. and 8.45p.m.

(Above): A view of Brill engine shed and the dilapidated forge.

London Transport Executive

(Below): On arrival at Brill, No. 41 replenishes its tanks at the water tank on Brill Shed. In charge is Neasden man, Bill Adams, who was, at this time, driver or passed fireman. The system of a weekly rota for engines No. 23 and No. 41 was that the engines would exchange at Quainton on a Sunday, and the engine leaving the branch would work the No. 6 goods train from Quainton back to Neasden.

D. W. K. Jones

Embellished tank side — London Transport No. 23 looks back from remotest regions of the system in the direction of its return to Quainton Road Station and the vacant locomotive shed. The smaller older shed nearby has now lost its set of rails.

Roy Slaymaker Collection

Engine No. 23 was the elder sister of the two Brill engines, and was originally an A class engine of the 1864-70 construction period. She also retained much of her original form, the condensing pipes being a continual reminder, in the open air, that this was once an underground engine. Alongside the sloping semi-circular smokebox door was the rod controlling the condensing valves, link-rodded back to the cab. The short upright pipe on the tank tops was to release exhaust vapour when the circulating water in the tanks became very hot. By comparison, in this book, it can be seen that the other engine, No. 41, was one of a batch that had the condensing equipment removed. The first of the class to be withdrawn was No. 1, which ran into the buffers at Baker Street in 1897, and was damaged beyond repair. With electrification of city lines from 1905 to 1907, two-thirds of the class left their indigenous regions for scrapping or for other railways. By 1913, the last of that section of the class that had originally been Class B were dispensed with. By the time the LPTB took over the Metropolitan Railway in 1933, only five remained of the one-time sixty six; the two Brill engines and Nos. 27, 48 and 49. No. 48 was also photographed on Brill line duty. Many of the class had worked goods trains between Aylesbury and Verney Junction after displacement from passenger duty by Class E engines. They, in turn, replaced the D class on Brill line trains by 1915.

Lens of Sutton

Brill No. 1 at the platform end at Brill, with one wagon and the early Metropolitan straight-sided coach. It is believed to be this vehicle that ran back from Brill to Wotton in the incident related by Jack Roberts in the chapter entitled 'The Tram'.

Mike Horne Collection

WOTTON TRAMWAY.

HIS GRACE THE DUKE OF BUCKINGHAM AND CHANDOS, PROPRIETOR.

NOTICE.

From and after Monday, October 1st, the 5.55 p.m. Train, QUAINTON to BRILL, will be DISCONTINUED. A TRAIN INSTEAD will leave about 4.20 p.m.

R. A. JONES,

Brill, September 20th, 1888.

Manager.

G. T. DE FRAINE, "BUCKS HERALD" OFFICE, WALTON STREET, AYLESBURY.

(Above):   No. 23 shunts her stock at Brill in preparation for the return journey to Quainton.

L&GRP/Courtesy David & Charles

(Below):   A close-up view of the station board at Wood Siding, including the closure notice.

Lens of Sutton

CHAPTER FIVE

The Metropolitan Railway Between Aylesbury and Verney Junction

Bustling Aylesbury, as the driver of the Metropolitan H class puts the 'bag' in from the platform-end water-tower. In the frame of the station name-board, the carriage destination board, Verney Junction, can be seen.

H. C. Casserley

As already outlined in the first chapter, the railway from Aylesbury to Verney Junction was finally completed and opened on 23rd September 1868, and was the conclusion of a great deal of bitterness between the local railway promoters and the L&NWR. As a result of this, the line was put to hiring engines and rolling stock from the GWR who made an end-on connection with the line, and shared the same station in Aylesbury.

Things were allowed to continue this way for twenty six years, by which time another railway company had entered the sphere of Aylesbury railways. Shortly before that took place, came the death, on Thursday, 26th March 1889, of the Duke of Buckingham and Chandos, aged 65 years. Born 10th September 1823, Richard Plantagenet Campbell Temple-Nugent-Brydges-Chandos-Grenville, was Director of the Buckinghamshire Railway from 1853 until 1862; Chairman of The London & North Western Railway from 1853 to 1861; Chairman of the Aylesbury & Buckingham Railway and proprietor of the Wotton Tramway, and promoter of the Oxford, Aylesbury & Metropolitan Junction Railway. A special train brought the Duke's body from London to Quainton Road on Tuesday, 2nd April. It was first of all taken to Stowe then brought from Stowe to Wotton after the service for internment in the family mausoleum. 'At 3 o'clock the first special train

of mourners alighted five handsome carriages provided by the L&NWR at Church Siding which, when filled, left for Quainton Road Station. This was followed by a similar train containing the Bucks. Yeomanry which was attached to a normal GWR service for the journey to London'. It is fascinating to imagine what motive power was made available, possibly by the L&NWR, to haul the 'five handsome carriages' from Wotton to Quainton. A funereal task, but spectacular in exception for the Wotton Tramway.

The Metropolitan Railway opened their extension to Rickmansworth on 1st September 1889, in prospect of developing the popular homesteads for the commuter traffic in the Chilterns. Next came the opening of that section of the line that would bring them into the GWR and Aylesbury & Buckingham Railway station at Aylesbury. This was opened on 1st September 1892. The year before, by process of an Act of 25th July 1890, the A&BR was taken over by the Metropolitan Railway and the GWR's interests in the line thenceforth ceased. Included in this Act, which became law on 1st January 1894, were clauses to protect the interests of one Rt. Hon. William Stephen Temple, and the workings ,of the Wotton Tramway. The purchase price of the A&BR was £150,000.

With the absorption of the A&BR, the Metropolitan Railway were obliged to take in hand extensive alterations to what had, in effect, been nothing more than a very frugal single line country railway, not so far removed in status from the Wotton Tramway. The installation of double track along its entire length meant virtual rebuilding of the stations and ancillary structures. Included in this were the extensive alterations to Quainton Road Station, where a road crossing was to be closed and a bridge built over the line. This brought about the total resiting of the station itself, all completed by October, 1899.

The added complication at Quainton was the existence of the Wotton Tramway and its connection with the main line, which had been recently modified with a proper junction connection, rather than a siding running on to a small turntable. Nevertheless, with the new station platforms now covering some of the trackwork, the Tramway junction was perforce redesigned again.

The terminus station of Verney Junction was, ironically in view of Euston's early antipathies, rebuilt in conjunction with the L&NWR, and in that company's style. Extensive new exchange sidings were put in and, no doubt, both companies looked forward to an exchange of traffic at this potentially busy point.

After Edward Watkin's attempt to steer the Metropolitan beyond an outer suburban role, to become part of a main trunk route, had failed, his prospects with the Manchester, Sheffield & Lincolnshire Railway (later GCR) fared rather better. They obviously saw the extension of their system to the capital as a logical step in their development, although probably with some reservations of the grand Trans-Continental trunk line that Watkin perceived.

The Act for the new main line was secured on 28th March 1893; ninety nine miles from Annesley, near Sheffield, to the Metropolitan station of Quainton Road, and the hoped for acquiescence of this company for the further distance from there to Neasden. The line was opened for coal traffic on 25th July 1898, whilst the passenger service started from the company's own terminus at Marylebone Station on 15th March 1899.

Unfortunately, the ambitions of the GCR brought them into conflict with the Metropolitan on this shared causeway into London. As the last main line, it was regarded as an interloper, and it was only after the expense of a diverse arrangement with the GWR, for an alternative route which was constructed, that the two companies resolved their differences into the Metropolitan & Great Central Joint Committee. Conflict had grown, understandably enough, out of clearly separate ambitions. Metropolitan plans followed on the purchase of large tracts of agricultural land on each side of their extended route from London. Across these acres it was hoped would swell the new suburbia, filling heavily loaded daily commuter trains back and forth from the capital each working day, with a weekend leisure service. The movement of goods traffic would be a small mote compared to other railways, including the Great Central. Although these plans proved largely justified and fruitful, the area of North Buckinghamshire did not prove as attractive to the domestic taste. It therefore remained agricultural hinterland with its scattering of farms, though oddly industralised with occasional large brick factories. The Northern terminus, Verney Junction, was therefore resolved into little more than a small railway hamlet with a country inn. Exchange sidings put in there did, however, prove useful for goods traffic, especially in the period of the LMS and LNER. An alternative access to them was built during World War II after a junction was put in on the Oxford to Bletchley line of the LMS from the ex-GCR main line at Claydon, with a short connecting link.

(324)

M.R.

WENDOVER

TO

Verney Junc.

Returning to the period of the Metropolitan, the high water mark of their use of the A&BR line to Verney Junction was the initiation of a Pullman service, by introducing two brand-new cars to run between there and Baker Street on 1st June 1910. The Metropolitan Railway obviously took great pride in this service and issued much publicity to the effect. The Manager of the company, Mr R. H. Selbie, spoke proudly of the role played by British companies in producing these two beautiful vehicles. 'Aided by the art of Messrs W. S. Laycock Limited and the Birmingham Railway Carriage & Wagon Company Limited, these two palatial Pullmans *Mayflower* and *Galatea* are evolved to run between Aylesbury and Chesham on the Metropolitan Extension Railway and various stations on the Metropolitan Railway between Baker Street and Aldgate'.

Prior to the public service being brought into operation on 1st June 1910, an inaugural run was made with invited guests of the Metropolitan Railway on 27th May.

A description of the car is supplied in the *Railway and Travel Monthly* of 1910 and is a peroration of praise for this sumptuous age now vanished forever. 'The exteriors of the cars are finished in the standard Pullman colours, namely, umber bodies with the upper panels in white and tastefully lined with gold; the roofs are painted white and the underframes and bogies black'. 'The cars are divided into two large saloons, one capable of comfortably seating eight passengers and the other seven. There is also a smaller saloon at one end arranged to seat four; that latter compartment should prove very useful in the case of travellers requiring extra privacy, as it can be reserved and shut off entirely from the rest of the car. All the compartments are provided with tables, fitted with electric standard lamps and bell pushes. A well-fitted lavatory compartment is provided at one end. The end saloon contains a commodious buffet counter, behind which is a pantry fitted with a gas stove, hot and cold water and every convenience for the supply of refreshments'. 'The period of decoration used for the *Galatea* buffet car is that of the latter part of the 18th century'. 'The mural scheme is composed of fine fiddleback mahogany with the upper panels inlaid with satinwood on a ground of fine quartered and veneered fiddleback mahogany. There are eight flap tables in the car which have glass tops on which are placed electric lamps of chased design. Each compartment has a coved plaster ceiling with an ornamental band on the flat, forming a panel. From

(Above): A rare glimpse of Aylesbury Station in pre-Metropolitan days, when it was the terminus of the GWR Wycombe branch from Maidenhead, Wycombe and Princes Risborough; also the shared station of the Aylesbury & Buckingham Railway. The platform for the former company is on the left with the buildings, whilst the latter company platform is on the right.

Payne & Son

(Below): A view looking north from Aylesbury Station, showing the ex-GWR broad gauge goods shed, which was much closer to the station than the later shed that was situated a few hundred yards further north.

Payne & Son

this band are suspended the ceiling lights. Wall brackets are also fixed at suitable places on the wall panelling. The bell pushes, switches and number frames are of ormolu, finely chased and glided'. 'The blinds which are of green silk damask have been especially woven. Above each blind there is an ormolu baggage rack, with finely chased ornamentation and panels of brass treillage'.

'The floor is covered with deep green pile carpet and the chairs are luxuriously upholstered and covered with green morocco'.

'The upper panels of the cross partitions are of clear plate glass, thus enabling one to see from end to end of the car'.

'The style of the *Mayflower* buffet car is that of the Georgian period. The combination of the oak and holly makes a most

The public nightmare, for both passengers and company, the calamitous force of a locomotive ripped like paper, and coaches burst into smithereens. This terrible sight filtered through the grey dawn of Friday, 23rd December 1904, at Aylesbury Station after the 2.45a.m. parcels from Marylebone to Manchester took the 15m.p.h. restricted curve at Aylesbury, wildly in excess of that limit, at 3.45a.m., and brought the inevitable catastrophe. In the resulting inquiry by the Board of Trade, the Presiding Officer criticised the Great Central Railway after evidence suggesting that Driver Joseph Barnshaw of Openshaw, Manchester, was not sufficiently aware of the route between Leicester and London. A colleague remembered that he said, on being booked the train, that he had not been to London for twelve months. The Great Central countered this accusation by pointing out that Barnshaw had, in fact, travelled over the route some 278 times. Although on night duty, it was claimed that he had slept well and was a good driver with a clear record, the very essence of sobriety. Sadly, the truth that he could have imparted was denied the inquiry, as he died on that Friday night from his severe wounds, without properly regaining consciousness. It must be added, however, that the night in question was one of thick fog. The reason for lack of caution in an otherwise abstemious man must remain as one of the insoluble mysteries of railway lore, similar to the bewildering cataclysm at Grantham, two years later, in 1906. Other fatalities were Fireman George Masters and two railway officers travelling as passengers in the train.

S. G. Payne

Aylesbury Station, in the throes of track re-alignment and the rebuilding of the 'down' platform after the Aylesbury railway disaster. Note the A class engine in the distance in the 1903 condition, identical to that of the now preserved No. 23.

Bill George Collection

Pullman car *Mayflower*, photographed before entering service, unfortunately outside the age of colour photography. Nevertheless, the pristine elegance is fairly well evident. What a superb company image they must have presented as they gleamed back and forth through Aylesbury, Quainton Road and Verney Junction stations. The familiar Pullman livery did not, however, weather subterranean railways very well, and it was changed to all-over crimson lake in 1923. Dimensional details were as follows:

Length over buffers: 59ft.
Length over body: 57ft. 6in.
Width over footboards: 8ft. 8in.
Centres of bogies apart: 39ft. 3in.
Wheelbase of bogies: 7ft. 6in.

Wheel diameter: 3ft. 4⅝ in.
Width over body: 8ft. 5in.
Height from rail to top of roof: 12ft.
Weight: 29 tons
Seating capacity: 19 persons

Historical Model Railway Society

pleasing effect. The wall scheme is composed of panels of fine wainscot oak, with the upper panels inlaid with enrichments of the Georgian period on a ground of fine quartered and veneered oak'.

'The car is divided into three compartments with cross partitions. An excellent effect is obtained through clear plate glass having been fixed in the upper panels of these partitions. There are chairs for 19 persons in the car and patent hinged tables with plate glass tops are provided'.

'Each compartment has a coved plaster ceiling with an ornamental band on the flat, forming a panel. From this band are suspended the ceiling lights. Wall brackets are also fixed at suitable places on the wall panelling. The bell pushes, switches and number frames are of ormolu, finely chased and gilded. The blinds, which are of crimson silk damask, have been specially woven and above each blind there is an ormolu baggage rack with finely chased enrichments, with panels of brass treillage. The floor is covered with crimson deep pile carpeting and the chairs are luxuriously upholstered and covered with crimson morocco'.

'Whilst the interior woodwork of the cars differs, some of the decorative features are the same, namely the electric light fittings which, in addition to the ceiling light fittings, consist of wall brackets suitably disposed and table standards of brass, gilded by the mercurial process. Door handles, basket racks, ventilators and other fittings of chased and gilded brass have been specially designed and modelled to harmonise. It is certainly worthy of note that the cars are entirely British-built, the whole of the construction having been carried out in the works of the Birmingham Carriage & Wagon Company Ltd., at Smethwick. The interiors were designed by Messrs W. S. Laycock Ltd., and the entire construction has been to the approval of Mr C. Jones, the Metropolitan Railway

Locomotive & Carriage Superintendent, under the supervision of Mr Thomas Powell, Secretary and Manager of the Pullman Co. Ltd.'.

'With regard to the timetable, the first 'up' car is attached to the 8.30a.m. train from Aylesbury as one car is kept cn the siding there overnight. The train is non-stop to Amersham and Harrow, running right through to Aldgate, which it reaches at 9.59a.m. The second car making good the deficiency of the non-stop car, starts at 8.55a.m. from Chesham for Liverpool Street'.

'In the afternoon, except on Saturdays, cars leave Aylesbury at 1.35p.m. for Baker Street and at 4.15p.m. for Aldgate, and at 9.15p.m. from Verney Junction for Baker Street. To replace these on Saturdays a car leaves Verney Junction for Baker Street at 6p.m.'

'In the 'down' direction cars leave Aldgate at 10.07a.m. and Baker Street at 12.05p.m., from Aldgate at 5.22p.m. for Aylesbury while from Aldgate there is another at 6.08p.m. which runs through to Verney Junction. These are all withdrawn on Saturdays and cars at 1.30p.m. and 1.56p.m. from Aldgate are substituted; the latter running to Verney Junction.'

'A theatre train is also run every night during the week to Aylesbury, leaving Baker Street at 11.35p.m.'

'The cars are available for use by the holders of first class tickets, either single journey tickets or season tickets upon payment of an extra fee of 6d. (2½p) per passenger between London and Rickmansworth and intermediate stations and 1s. 0d. (5p) between London and the stations north of Rickmansworth.'

'This service is an interesting development of the facilities of outer suburban travel and we trust the commendable enterprise of the Metropolitan Railway and the Pullman Car Co. will meet the support it most certainly deserves.'

The invention of the motor car, in 1887, and the opening of

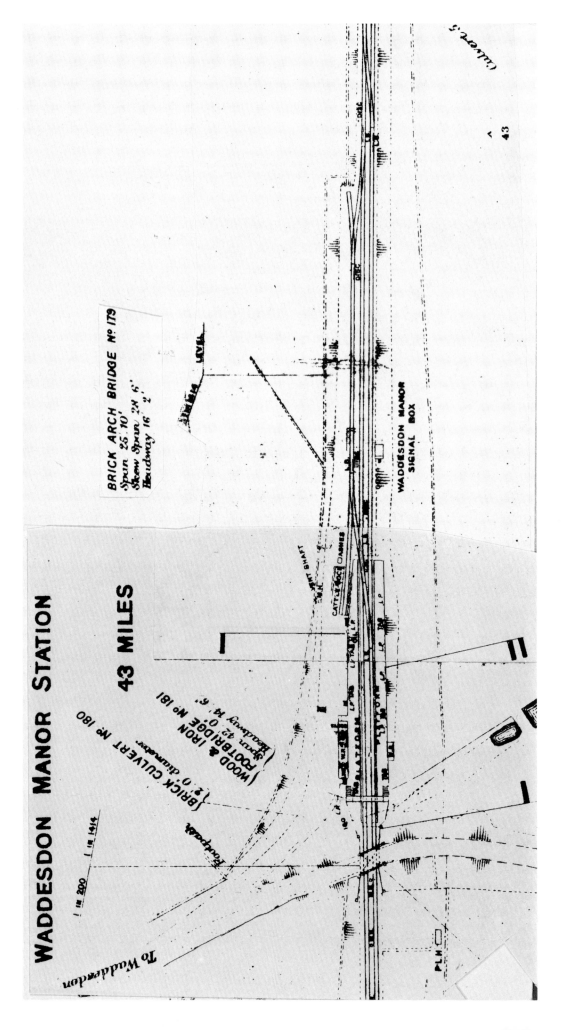

Waddesdon Manor Station, circa 1910.

Mike Crosbie

The luckless D class of the Metropolitan. Their compact form and short accommodating wheelbase suggests that they should be ideal for short haul branch line work. In reality, they became untrustworthy on passenger work, with a nasty predilection to blow-backs which put them almost permanently on goods work. Sister engine No. 75 compounded the class malaise by damaging the track at Brill on the very first visit up the branch. Just discernible on this print is a little of the cast number on the front of the chimney; an early method of numbering locomotives that endured on the Metropolitan.

R. C. Riley

the first electricity generating station in 1882 meant the release of two potent forces for change that would extensively alter the nature of railways. Railway companies became aware of this with the few vehicles that began to appear on Britain's roads in the first decade of the twentieth century, and the growth of town suburbs. Their answer was to introduce different vehicles called steam railmotors, which normally consisted of one steam motorised saloon coach operating along a sequence of lightly-constructed timber platforms called halts, with many stops and quick acceleration between journeys.

Although the system had some success, it did rather better with a more conventional arrangement of engine and specially-designed one or two coaches with the odd van added; these being called push-pull trains. The steam railmotors themselves proved too lightly-powered to haul more than their own coach body, which proved too limiting to be economically justifiable. It is the push-pull unit that found regular use on the Aylesbury

to Verney Junction line after the line was taken over by the Metropolitan. The first engines used were L&NWR, followed by a brief but ill-fated use of the new D class. Up until the amalgamation of railways in 1923, and the Metropolitan Railway's relinquishment of the service to the LNER, it was operated by the GCR locomotives at Aylesbury. From 1923, or thereabouts, through the circumstances of amalgamation, came the arrival of an ex-Great Eastern 0-6-0 tank engine, a Class J71. This engine, along with ex-GCR tank No. 5594, continued to work the service until closure.

After World War I, the competition between road and rail lost its genteel whiff of mild skirmishing, and was thrown into top gear. Thousands of trucks, buses and motor vehicles that had carried the armies to France became demobbed and purchased for private use. Together with so many men taught to drive them, the inevitable happened and small carrier and bus fleets mushroomed all over the country during the 1920s.

A change of ownership to the LNER can in no way diminish those famous lines of the handsome Robinson Atlantics of the Great Central Railway. No. 6090 pauses with an 'up' express train at Aylesbury on 22nd June 1935.

H. C. Casserley

(Below): Grandborough Road Station and goods siding.

Mike Crosbie

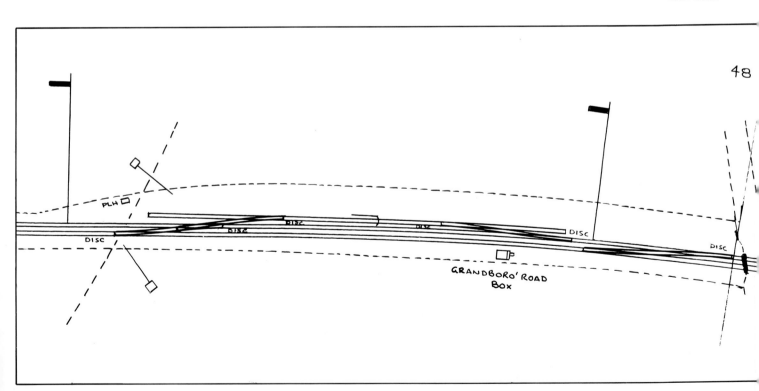

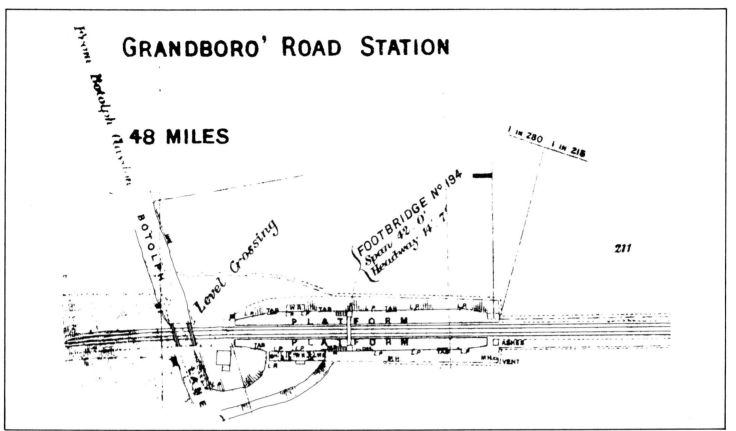

GRANDBORO' ROAD STATION

48 MILES

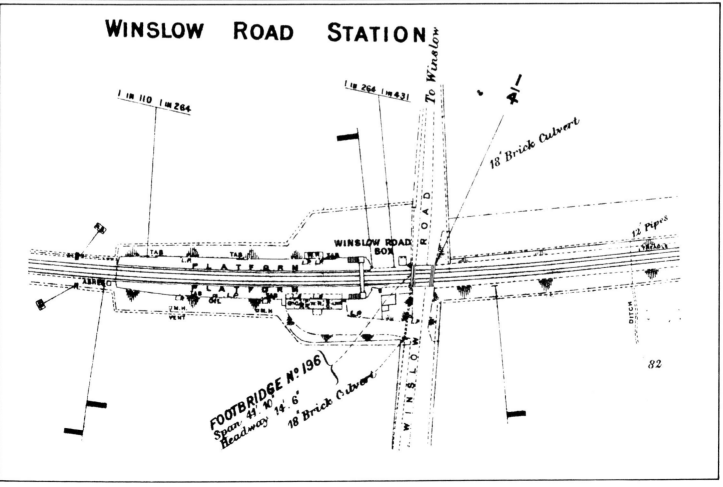

WINSLOW ROAD STATION

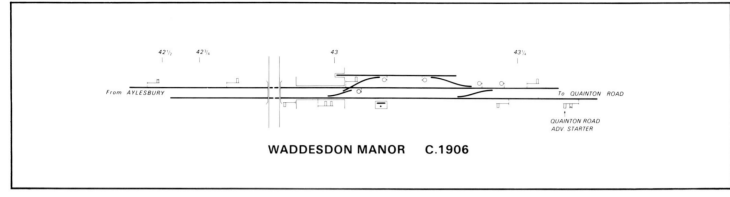

42½   42¾   43   43¼

From AYLESBURY   To QUAINTON ROAD

QUAINTON ROAD
ADV. STARTER

WADDESDON MANOR   C.1906

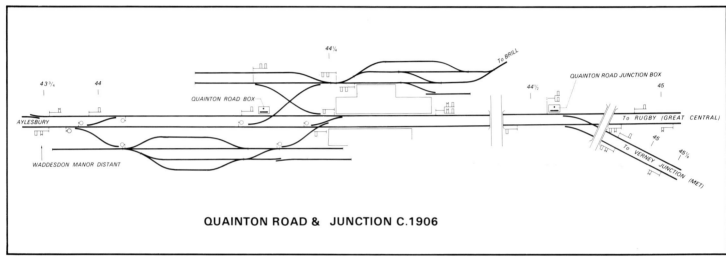

44¼   To BRILL

QUAINTON ROAD JUNCTION BOX

43¾   44   44½   45

QUAINTON ROAD BOX

AYLESBURY   To RUGBY (GREAT CENTRAL)

45

WADDESDON MANOR DISTANT   To VERNEY JUNCTION (MET) 45¼

QUAINTON ROAD & JUNCTION C.1906

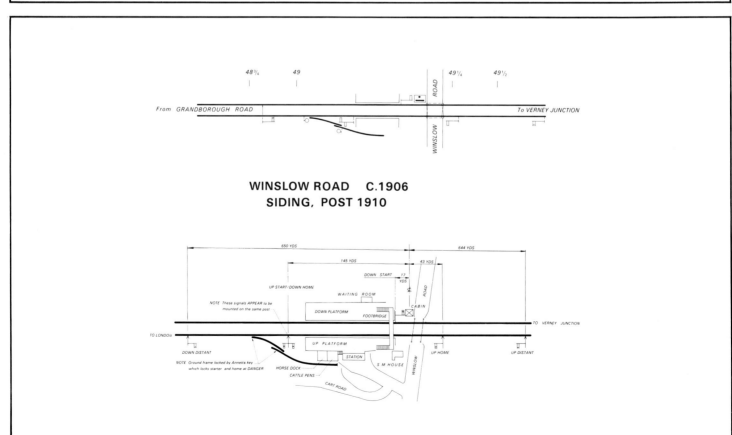

48¾   49   49¼   49½

ROAD

From GRANDBOROUGH ROAD   To VERNEY JUNCTION

WINSLOW

WINSLOW ROAD   C.1906
SIDING, POST 1910

650 YDS   644 YDS

145 YDS   43 YDS

DOWN START 17
           YDS

UP START/DOWN HOME

WAITING ROOM

NOTE These signals APPEAR to be
mounted on the same post

DOWN PLATFORM   CABIN

        FOOTBRIDGE   TO VERNEY JUNCTION

TO LONDON

                 UP PLATFORM

DOWN DISTANT   UP HOME   UP DISTANT

NOTE Ground frame locked by Annetts key   STATION
   which locks starter and home at DANGER   S M HOUSE
          HORSE DOCK   WINSLOW
         CATTLE PENS
           CART ROAD   CART ROAD

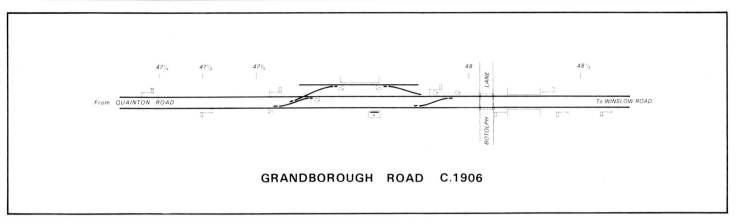

GRANDBOROUGH ROAD C.1906

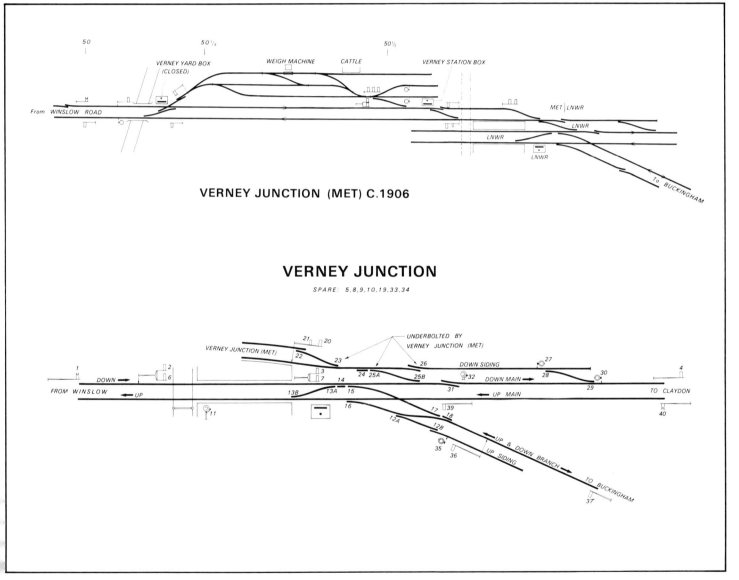

VERNEY JUNCTION (MET) C.1906

VERNEY JUNCTION

SPARE: 5,8,9,10,19,33,34

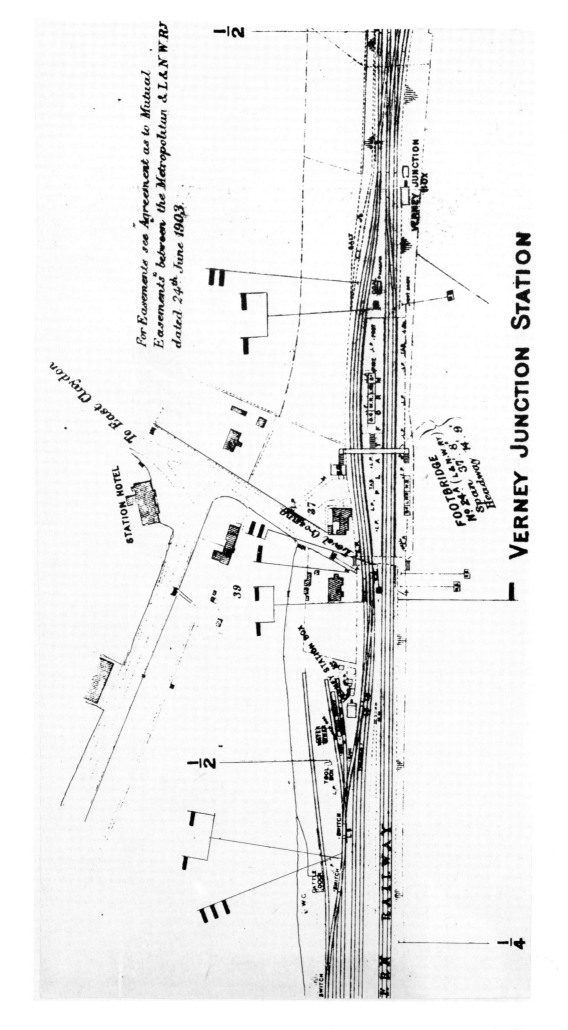

VERNEY JUNCTION STATION

Mike Crosbie

The ground plan of the remote Verney Junction. The Bletchley to Oxford line runs across the site, from left to right, and Metropolitan lines enter by the sidings on the left and run alongside the outer face of the island platform. The branch to Banbury starts to curve from the rails into the Oxford direction on the extreme right, a tacit connection through one set of points, with the L&NWR just to the right of that company's signal box. Verney Junction box. The Verney Station box of the Metropolitan stands adjacent to two short sidings that were the Verney Sidings. The only building of any significance apart from the station is the Station Hotel.

The Aylesbury to Verney Junction motor train at Aylesbury in the 1930s, in the charge of ex-GCR 2-4-2 tank engine No 5594.

Lens of Sutton

(Below): Aylesbury Town Station steam shed, which once had a hectic concentration of motive power for such a restricted site, which was how it remained from its early broad gauge days, when merely at the end of a branch from Princes Risborough. Other developments brought its use by the Metropolitan and GCR, in addition to the GWR. It became exclusively standard gauge in 1868 with the opening of the Aylesbury & Buckingham Railway. At that time, there was a turntable just about where the engine is standing in the photograph. It was not originally a through running shed, the rear wall being removed and sliding doors being put in sometime after 1940. The engine is standing alongside the coaling stage that is still covered by the bracket and pillar supports which once held the small water tank of mid-nineteenth century vintage. The limitation of this probably brought the construction of the much larger tank near the shed which, incidentally, was built over a well. Details of the structure are that it was brick-built, and originally had a slated northern lit saw-tooth roof pattern. It measured 150ft. x 33ft., with offices and stores building 80ft. x 15ft. As a GWR shed, it was a sub-shed to Slough, and had a locomotive supplied from Banbury to work the Princes Risborough to Banbury service. Under the Metropolitan, the shed became a sub-shed to Neasden (34E), which is how it remained until closure in the early 1960s. Further details are recounted in the chapter 'The Tram' by engine driver Bill Fry, and for later days by Jack Turner.

British Rail

Pride of the Great Central, a Robinson Atlantic, heads south through Waddesdon Manor Station early this century. A particular anomaly amongst the group of buildings along the Aylesbury to Verney Junction line, is that the Waddesdon Station buildings are on the 'down' side of the line, whereas all the buildings on the other stations are on the 'up'.

Bill George Collection

The Verney Junction to Aylesbury motor train runs into Waddesdon Station, in the 1930s, with one cattle van attached to the rear.

London Transport Executive

A view of the motor train, seen as it steams away to Verney, looking from the carriage of an 'up' train, on 2nd May 1936. Note the crossover mid-way along the platform and the single name of 'Waddesdon', as 'Manor' was dropped in 1922.

H. C. Casserley

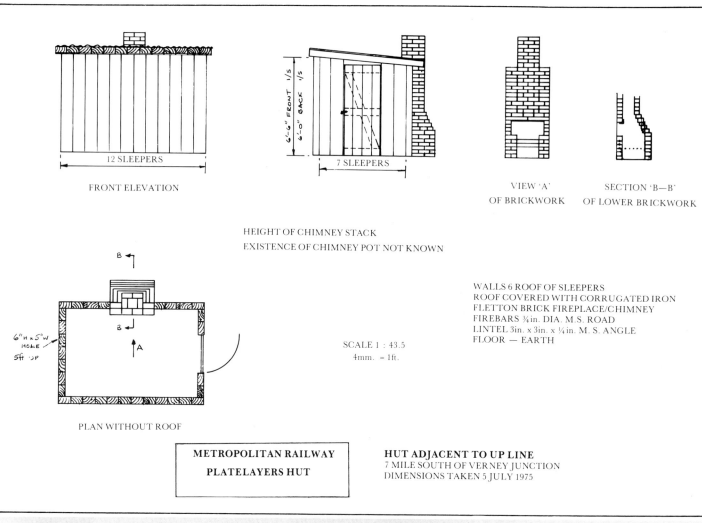

FRONT ELEVATION

12 SLEEPERS

7 SLEEPERS

6'-6" FRONT I/S
6'-0" BACK I/S

VIEW 'A'
OF BRICKWORK

SECTION 'B—B'
OF LOWER BRICKWORK

HEIGHT OF CHIMNEY STACK
EXISTENCE OF CHIMNEY POT NOT KNOWN

B

B

A

6"H x 5"W
HOLE
5ft UP

PLAN WITHOUT ROOF

SCALE 1 : 43.5
4mm. = 1ft.

WALLS 6 ROOF OF SLEEPERS
ROOF COVERED WITH CORRUGATED IRON
FLETTON BRICK FIREPLACE/CHIMNEY
FIREBARS ¾ in. DIA. M.S. ROAD
LINTEL 3 in. x 3 in. x ¼ in. M. S. ANGLE
FLOOR — EARTH

METROPOLITAN RAILWAY
PLATELAYERS HUT

HUT ADJACENT TO UP LINE
7 MILE SOUTH OF VERNEY JUNCTION
DIMENSIONS TAKEN 5 JULY 1975

Quainton Road, with flower beds and sunshine in the 1920s.

London Transport Executive

On 15th March 1930, ex-GCR tank No. 5594 proceeds on its way to Aylesbury with the local push-pull service, calling at Quainton Road.

H. C. Casserley

The camera blink of a frozen moment fifty years ago when the line between Aylesbury and Verney Junction was due for closure to passenger traffic, although the scene would not suggest that. The motor train is under the charge of the 0-6-0 Holden ex-GER tank No. 8307, the final engine to perform this duty. The oil or paraffin can gives a pleasant period flavour, whilst driver and porter are obviously discussing the contents of the luggage van. The conglomeration of bikes on the 'up' platform have probably been left by local commuters. A few schoolgirls wait — they may well be amongst the many that have spoken with affection nowadays of what they regarded as their own little railway that ran between Quainton and Brill.

London Transport Executive

This view shows the continuation of the same building pattern for the Aylesbury to Verney Junction line at Grandborough Road.

London Transport Executive

Grandborough Road, with the same train as the Quainton photograph. Removal of poster boards and the overall emptiness suggests that this could be close to the final day, although patronage is still evident. A particular difference at Grandborough was the 'up' platform which was of concrete whilst the 'down' side was of the familiar brick. Behind the carriage is the crossing keeper's house, and the gates appear to be having some attention on the right.

London Transport Executive

Two views, north and south, at Winslow Road, as rebuilt by the Metropolitan Railway. The addition of the 'down' platform leaves the small signal box rather poorly sited, which is unusual for the attentiveness required of the signalman.

L&GRP/Courtesy David & Charles and London Transport Executive

A remarkable print of a section of the original A&BR station at Winslow Road. Early track is flat bottom and flange-bolted. As it was at this time, the single line in the foreground rails would be of a siding. Comparison with the Metropolitan period photographs will reveal that the platform was entirely rebuilt. There are various curiosities of the period including the small hut for the gatekeeper/porter with his dwelling nearby. The gates themselves appear to be of iron, in fine frame; they were later replaced by timber. The lamp on the post next to the man is interesting. This could possibly rotate with green and red lenses to effect request stops for some of the trains.

London Transport Executive

The railway monopoly was now seriously on the defensive. Also, after the war, the Metropolitan Railway reintroduced the Pullman service after its suspension during hostilities. It was to be a kind of 'St. Martin's summer' for these beautiful vehicles now in all crimson livery. Although they terminated at Aylesbury, the service lasted until 7th October 1939 when again, the war brought it to a close. They were then sold out of stock and were used for a final ten years as a wood merchant's office buildings in Surrey.

A small note of particular change during the 1920s was that the 'Manor' part of the Waddesdon Manor Station was dropped on 1st October 1922. To avoid confusion, the Waddesdon on the Brill line was then changed to Waddesdon Road.

With the formation of the LPTB in 1933 came the withdrawal of Metropolitan interest north of Aylesbury, relinquishing this to the LNER, who found little enthusiasm beyond the ex-GCR main line. Closure notices were posted for the Quainton to Verney section passenger service for 4th July 1936. Although Waddesdon Station was not in this section, it was decided to close it at the same time. On 28th January 1940, Quainton Road to Verney Junction was converted to single track, using the 'up' line. The 'down' line was left as a long

siding from Verney Junction to Winslow Road. Goods traffic would still continue in varying levels of activity until 6th September 1947. A wartime intensity developed involving the sidings at Verney Junction which was circuited into part of the diversionary route around London and, for this purpose, a link was put in at Claydon with the GCR line and the Oxford & Bletchley line; this was called Claydon Junction. A remarkable exception to the cessation of Metropolitan services on this line was its reopening from 1943 to 1948 to Quainton; but all use of the line finally ceased in 1957 and the rails were eventually lifted in 1961. The siding from Verney was used for some time for wagon storage.

With the nationalisation of the railways in 1948, and the formation of British Railways, the tempo of the Old Great Central main line was maintained with powerful A2 and A3 classes hauling north country and East Midland expresses, including the 'Master Cutler', a businessman's train from Marylebone to Sheffield, daily.

However, with the publication of the modernisation plan in 1955, and the Beeching cataclysm of 1962 that followed it, there was no long term future for this manifest portion of Watkin's great dream of a main line and channel tunnel railway to the

A member of the mighty K class, No. 112, at Verney Junction on 2nd May 1936. This was the largest engine of the Metropolitan, which the London Transport did not retain for long, for with the advancing electrification, and the closure of the north of Aylesbury service, they were sold to the LNER who classified them in their list as L2, working from the GCR shed at Neasden. They continued working the goods trains between Finchley Road, Rickmansworth and Aylesbury after the closure of the line to Verney Junction. This did not, however, continue for long, as the first engine to be scrapped, No. 112, seen here, went in January 1943 with the other five following close behind over five subsequent years, tragically youthful (1923), but out of accord with LNER standardisation.

H. C. Casserley

Continent. Closure came in 1963, followed by track lifting in 1968. A line of only 67 years, with beautifully engineered sweeping earthworks and long vaulting arched viaducts formed the despair of an unrequited ideal; a route of Romanesque directness pointing emptily into the horizon.

The portion of the line from Marylebone to Aylesbury is still retained for suburban services, whilst the section from Aylesbury to Quainton Road, and up to the wartime connection at Claydon, is still used by British Rail for various trains, predominantly to fulfil a contract with the London Brick Company for container trains of London's domestic rubbish from Hillingdon to the worked-out Calvert Works claypits, to fill and surface them with soil for farmland. Brick trains ceased operating from the company siding in December 1977. Occasional passenger trains of railway enthusiasts also pass over these metals, especially on the open days of the Quainton Railway Preservation Society, when well-filled diesel multiple units bring visitors to the steam days and to view the surviving station of Quainton Road, or ride behind a steam locomotive-hauled train from its platform, and possibly muse upon a time when they could have got off their train and booked another to take them to the village of Brill.

The remainder of the A&BR line to Verney Junction is a mere overgrown trackbed, through cutting and over embankment, with the raised humps of weedy platforms. Verney itself was a hardy survivor, even a year beyond the other station that carried the other family name of Calvert, for as a result of the later closure of the Oxford to Bletchley line in 1967, Verney could claim the laurel wreath of longevity before it finally succumbed to the grassy thrusts of broken brickwork and masonry. The link of the GW & GC Joint Committee from Grendon Underwood to Ashendon Junction also managed to survive, in part, from Grendon to the site of Akeman Street Station, as this is still in use for the Westcott Fertiliser Works.

In keeping with most surviving stations of the present day, Aylesbury is a great deal more subdued than in its past. There is a slender passenger service which still runs on the old branch of the Wycombe Railway, once the preserve of broad gauge trains, to Princes Risborough, mainly for schoolchildren, whilst the main link with the metropolis still has its commuter rushes, which are catered for by inveterate diesel multiple units between periods of silence and immobility.

As a footnote, the old rival, the Aylesbury Railway from Cheddington was consigned to an early end in 1953, pre-empting the Beeching era.

It is gratifying to be able to write that the story of the Aylesbury & Buckingham Railway, the Metropolitan and the Great Central Railways, do not end so abruptly in the area. The burden of this cherished heritage has been taken up with determination and a great deal of sweat by volunteers, for whom railways and all they mean is an essential part of life itself. These groups, forming societies of like-minds not only resisted decline, but set about to preserve something of the great age of railways for future generations to enjoy. Happily, such a group became based at Quainton Road Station when final closure under British Railways' ownership came on 4th March 1963 for passenger traffic, and July 1966 for the goods yard. Thenceforth, the main line was singled, up to the connection with the Oxford to Bletchley line at Claydon Junction.

The origins of the Quainton Railway Society are rooted in the late 1950s, shortly after the obvious effects of the 1955 modernisation plan that were beginning to gain momentum, and many things familiar were leaving the railway scene, most dramatically, the decline of steam power and ascendancy of diesel and electric traction.

The first relics were acquired by the parent group, The London Railway Preservation Society, in 1963, and these eventually found a home at Quainton, in the spring of 1969. Adopting the name of the station, the new society was formed out of the old, which was wound up in 1971. Out of the barest beginnings, on a site that was without water and electricity, the society developed and expanded on the hard work of its volunteers and public support of its open days.

Nowadays, there is the regular business of running the steam locomotives, with a 'special rides' train, whilst work goes on with restoration of both engines and rolling stock. The society have the largest concentration of L&NWR stock in the country.

Quainton Station itself, although with a single line of rails, still remains as a perfect example of the Metropolitan's extended line into Buckinghamshire, and the style of station adopted for the Aylesbury to Verney Junction section. Occasionally it receives passenger trains again, with visiting railtours of other societies, or on the now familiar Quainton shuttle, run by British Rail on Quainton's open days and called, appropriately enough, 'The Quaintonian.' To anyone with a cherished view of railways, it is always a moment of singular pleasure to look down from the road bridge that leads to the ancient village and see beneath, an old station, very much filled with life, and a branch line train steaming patiently and waiting for passengers, as it has done since 1871.

The Metropolitan Railway platform face at Verney Junction. After a journey of just over fifty miles, the train would connect with the Oxford to Bletchley and Cambridge service of the L&NWR, and also the branch to Buckingham and Banbury. For its size, the station was curiously isolated. It did not exist before 1868 when the L&NWR had run their Oxford and Banbury trains from Winslow, a few miles down the line in the Bletchley direction. With the adjunct of the A&BR from that date, a station was formed alongside little more than a farmstead, and later developed further by the rebuilding jointly by the Metropolitan and L&NWR. Unlike many junctions, it never developed beyond the cross of lines, and remains merely a small hamlet with a public house sporting the name 'Verney Arms'. There was a short siding at the station, exclusively for the use of Claydon House, the home of the Verney family. This was probably for coal. Surprisingly now, the footbridge was not built until a great deal of pressure was brought to bear from local interests led by Sir Edmund Verney. In a letter of 23rd January 1895, he said that the people using the station were 'exposed to peril of their lives', especially crossing the near tracks of the Metropolitan; a porter had been killed on these in December 1893. The company countered that the line did not carry sufficient traffic to warrant a footbridge. At that time, there were four trains turning at Verney Junction from Aylesbury, with one afternoon luggage train from the station. Within a few years, the Baker Street service was added to the Aylesbury trains, which would intensify traffic to the point where a footbridge would be insisted upon by the Board of Trade.

London Transport Executive

A moment to pause for the camera at Verney Junction for the ex-GER (now LNER) 2-4-2 tank, together with its driver. It fell to No. 8307 to operate the passenger service on the final day, an elegiac close to the line that remained a country railway.

Lens of Sutton

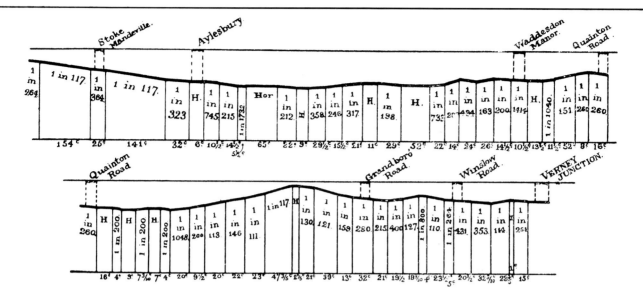

The gradient profile for the line from Aylesbury to Verney Junction. From Aylesbury to Quainton there is little of note and after a short rise at Quainton the progress becomes rather more taxing to climb up the section called Hogshaw Bank, which takes the line over Quainton Hill with a short section of 1 in 111, and on the opposite side 1 in 110.

Mike Horne Collection

STATION YARD WORKING, AYLESBURY STATION.

In order to ensure the punctual start of Up Passenger Trains from Aylesbury Station, the Verney Junction Rail Motor or Shuttle Train may, when necessary, be allowed to work up to the rear of a passenger train standing at the Up platform, and this must be done in accordance with Special Instructions shewn at end of Block Regulations at Aylesbury.

A D class engine, No. 75, used for working the goods north of Aylesbury to Verney Junction and on the Brill branch, seen here alongside Aylesbury Shed, early in the century.

R. C. Riley Collection

(Above):   The small signal box at Winslow Road, looking towards Verney Junction in 1934.

L. Harding

(Below):   An interior view, showing the thirty two lever frame at Grandborough Road.

L. Harding

CHAPTER SIX

'The Tram'

Miss Mary Varney, porter and gatekeeper at Westcott Station, takes her place with the irascible Harry Cross and his fireman, Arthur Bayliss. Miss Varney's brother also worked on the Tramway, and became stationmaster at Waddesdon Manor Station when it opened. He returned to the Tramway in 1917 with the responsibility for three stations; Waddesdon, Westcott and Wotton. He finally retired in 1930. The Varney family had substantial links with the Tramway; Miss Varney's father had been foreman platelayer on the line. The saddle tank engine is clearly recognisable as another product of the Boyne Engine Works in Leeds. It is in fact *Brill No. 1*, carrying the original name of *Earl Temple*. Arriving at the Tramway in December 1894, it was the second Manning Wardle engine to be purchased for the line by the O&AT., the first being *Huddersfield*. The change of name is possibly due to the purchase of the engine by the Metropolitan Railway. Its last known location was with Perry & Co., of Bow, in 1929. The livery is possibly a dark green, similar to Brunswick green, with broad black lines edged in yellow or orange. Although intended as contractors' engines they were, nevertheless, of attractive design.

Quainton Railway Society

A railway like the one to Brill was totally without pretention. It was about as basic as a railway could get, whilst still operating something of a regular timetable and fulfilling the requirements of local goods traffic. The original Chairman of the line was not ensconced within some lofty edifice of stone in faraway London, but lived near Wotton Underwood; palatially, it is true. His agent, the General Manager. R. A. Jones, also lived near the line at Brill, and everyone from that tier of authority downwards lived somewhere near the line and came from local communities. Therefore, it can be said that it was not only structurally basic but basic in the communal sense, a highly personable association with the people that it served. This lasted for many years until the adoption of running by the Metropolitan Railway brought in a strand of plutocracy. This was resisted as much as possible, and when people were sent from other parts of the railway to work on the line they soon became innured by its unique and unorthodox ways.

It would therefore be a fallacious thing to write any account of this railway in isolation of the local community, not to say divesting it of a rich and unique part of its existence. Therefore, this chapter looks at the Tramway through the eyes of the people that worked it, rode on it, or simply worked in one of the many nearby fields through which it passed on its familiar journeys.

The Third Duke of Buckingham was born 10th September 1823, and was the only son of the second Duke of Buckingham. He was christened Richard Plantagenet Campbell-Temple-Nugent-Brydges-Chandos-Grenville. He was Earl Temple until 1839 when he became the Marquess of Chandos on the death of his grandfather, the First Duke.

The Marquess of Chandos became Chairman of the London & North Western Railway from October 1853 until 1861. In that year, his father died, whereupon he became the Third Duke of Buckingham.

The Duke took a keen interest in railways from their early

A fragmentary glimpse of the earliest employee at Wood Siding, Mr Alfred Roberts. After twenty four years in the Army, serving mostly in India, Alfred Roberts retired from the service and took up his post at Wood Siding in 1892. Living nearby in Waterloo Cottages, he was employed at this spot handling many early morning milk consignments, that made use of the little station. He left the station to continue with sundry employment on estate farms in 1913.

Mrs Busby

Thomas Wilkins, who came for employment as a guard on the Tramway in 1881, from Gawcott near Buckingham. He lived with his wife and four children in one of the cottages at Brill Station. Eventually, whilst still a young man, he was promoted to clerk-in-charge at Brill. This was also something of a palliative, as he suffered from chronic consumption, and was hardly able to withstand exposure to the winter weather on the Brill line. Tragically, the malady was to culminate in his early death at the age of 34, on 13th February 1904.

Mrs Young

days and appeared to seek closer involvement with them. An interesting anecdote recounted in G. P. Neele's *Railway Reminiscences* (1904) shows that the Duke was not without a sense of humour as he would tease the L&NWR Board by repeating the following experience at more than one public function; an inci-

dent at Euston in the offices of the Superintendent of the line Mr Bruyeres, who had held this position since 1850.

Mr Bruyeres' chief clerk, a Mr Watts, received an unaristocratic looking personage entering and asking if he could see Mr Bruyeres.

'No, he was out.'

'I want to see him.'

'No doubt, but he is out.'

I particularly wanted to see him.'

'Yes many people do, but I know what you want . . . a job on the line. I may at once tell you you won't do . . . you're altogether too short!'

'Oh, perhaps you will give Mr Bruyeres this card and say I should have liked to have seen him.'

Watts looked at the card . . . the Marquess of Chandos! Tableau! poor Watts. He told me he shook in his shoes and wondered how soon his dismissal would be announced.

The same day his Lordship mused over being offered the position of Chairman, which he accepted, though he had just

A familiar name in the district was Washington, and reference to the list of employees in 1894 includes the man in the foreground here, Arthur Washington, working with two colleagues on the siding points at the Brill side of Wotton Station. A spot almost within sight of where the men are standing was the scene of tragedy, for it was there, between Wotton Station and the 'black tank', that a maid of Baroness Kinloss, daughter of the Duke of Buckingham, was knocked down and fatally injured by the engine on 8th March 1883. After an inquest, a verdict of accidental death was returned. Ellen Mary Nikalls was interred in Wotton Churchyard, only a short distance from where she fell.

S. W. A. Newton/Leicester County Council

been told, on what he supposed good authority, that he was not fit for porter!

It is rare that one can include the entire list of paid staff of a railway company. In the case of the Tramway, it is not only possible but serves to reflect the familiar nature of the close community of estate employment. Many of the people here are from families that have been in the area long before the Tramway came. In the case of the Varneys, Roberts and Washingtons, more than one member of the family was employed and often over more than one generation. This list, on *page 116*, is understood to be the entire staff, shortly before they became re-employed as staff on the Metropolitan Railway.

Jack Roberts, retired stationmaster of Rickmansworth, and formerly Wendover, served as a railwayman all his working life. Before the rank of stationmaster he had passed through the grades of signalman at various locations on the Metropolitan Railway. He began his working life at Fenemore's Foundry at Brill, but left there to work as a lad porter at the station in December 1914, working fifty hours each week for 8s. (40p). He remembers the staff at the station, in particular James

Hilsden who kept two dozen bantams in the vicinity of the station. He also remembers the mournful duty carried out with other local railwaymen, carrying the old stationmaster's coffin through the streets of Brill for three-quarters of a mile to the churchyard. James Hilsden had retired in 1923. One of the most striking things that he remembered about Brill Station was the congestion and collection of so many milk carts early in the morning, sometimes as many as thirty. Most of the carts would be well-loaded with the 17 gallon conical churns that were collected on the platform, and loaded into three milk vans that were attached to a passenger coach to make up the first train of the day. The vans tended to go to Marylebone, Aylesbury and Neasden, and a great deal of milk went to the Nestle's Milk Factory at Aylesbury.

Coal usually came in 4 to 5 wagon loads a week, whilst livestock was handled in varying amounts, with 4 to 5 vans per evening going down the line. The extraordinary composition of four vans loaded with cattle, together with a passenger coach, could present an unfavourable association on the windward side for the passengers. The enormous quantities of hay that went

Traffic				
Brill	Stevens, W.	Fitter	42s. 0d.	(£ 2.10p)
	Cross, H.	Driver	30s. 0d.	(£ 1.50p)
	Guntrip, R.	Stoker	15s. 0d.	(0.75p)
	Andrews, H.	Guard	18s. 0d.	(0.90p)
	Payne, W.	Carman	19s. 0d.	(0.95p)
Wotton	Smith, T.	Clerk-in-charge	14s. 0d.	(0.70p)
Quainton	Webb, A.	In charge of points	5s. 0d.	(0.25p)
Permanent Way				
Brill	Probats, I.	Platelayer	15s. 0d.	(0.75p)
	Washington, A.	Platelayer	15s. 0d.	(0.75p)
Wood Siding	Roberts, A.	Wood Siding Gatekeeper	10s. 0d.	(0.50p)
Westcott	Varney, W.	Foreman Platelayer	21s. 0d.	(£ 1.05p)
	Figg, D.	Platelayer	15s. 0d.	(0.75p)
	Washington, W.	Platelayer	15s. 0d.	(0.75p)
	Varney, Mrs I.	Gatekeeper	5s. 0d.	(0.25p)
Waddesdon	Varney, I.	Gatekeeper	10s. 0d.	(0.50p)
Quainton	Hammond, I.	Gatekeeper	5s. 0d.	(0.25p)
Salaried Staff				
Brill	Jones, R. A.	General Manager	£16. 13s. 4d.	(£16.66p)
	Wilkins, T.	Clerk-in-charge	£ 5. 16s. 8d.	(£ 5.83½p)
Waddesdon	Strong, H. J.	Clerk-in-charge	£ 5. 16s. 8d.	(£ 5.83½p)
	Hudson, I.	Rates, Audit and Correspondence	£ 6. 13s. 4d.	(£ 6.66½p)

Alfred Roberts' place at Wood Siding was taken by Benny Witchert, seen in this photograph, on the right, holding the red and green flags with which he could stop or wave the trains to continue. The Wood Siding Station board on his left is of an early period, and did not originally carry poster boards, the additional weight of which appears to have upset the foundation posts. The ladder in the Wood Siding oak is intriguing, and seems likely to be of a permanent arrangement whereby Benny would be able to sight the 'up' trains for some distance before their arrival at Wood Siding. Note the station name in the lantern glass of the lamp.

Mrs Busby

A good humoured parody of the 'Tram' by F. H. Stingemore. A modern refrain to this dance tune could certainly echo, that after fifty years since the line was 'through', its life and character is still popularly expressed to this day.

F. H. Stingemore

The pen of T. Tindell Wildridge portrays rather more bucolic somnolence at Westcott in the period of about 1908.

Roy Slaymaker Collection

A Elizabethan post-box for a Victorian station. The first post-box was
erected at Brill Station in 1904.

Author's Collection

down the line during World War I gave the impression that the
local farming community was feeding the horses of the entire
British Expeditionary Force. Added to this was Fenemore's
high demand for timber, that was being brought down the line
and into their siding, and one got the impression that the twenty
years preceding closure of the branch must have been the busiest
in its history. Jack did mention one mishap in all this movement
that he vividly remembered, with the vacuum brake isolated
off on the passenger coach. When this was uncoupled to run the
engine round at Brill, the guard had not applied the hand brake
fully, the coach decided to make its return independent of the
engine and ran backwards unrestrained until the gradient finally ceased its transports near Wotton Station. Ironically the
gates at Wood Siding had been removed by collision a week
earlier.

One small reference regarding the Aveling Porter engines
that had left the Brill line long before his arrival was that the
older men of his youth mentioned this strange machine to him,
Old Chainey, and they reckoned that you would never mistake it,
as it seemed to sound through the countryside for miles around
as it rattled along.

One Jack Bunyan, a distant relative of the famous religious
writer also came from Brill, and remembered, during his child-
hood, watching the men coming back from World War I at the
station. He used to wait when he knew that a number were
expected in the hope that they may have some souvenir to show.
He remarked that the men were still caked in Flanders' mud
when they got off the train, and when he approached them one
of them said, 'Don't come too close lad, or you may catch a few
lodgers'.

Mrs Brown of Oakley remembered how cold the train was in
winter; there never seemed to be any heating switched on.
However, all her memories do not have the same chill, for she
has special affection for those languid days of summer when you
could sit and cool your feet through the windows of the train,
and there never seemed any danger of catching them on anything as the train went so slow rolling over open fields, with no
lineside obstructions. As the train was being run over the crossing at Wood Siding, Driver Arthur Bayliss and the guard would
take even more time to perform the task, allowing the children
to get off the train and pick flowers in the wood for a botany
lesson! And if you should lose your hat, Arthur would stop the
train and pick it up on the way back, making sure that you got
it back as soon as possible. She also remembered the shine and
sparkle of the engine which was so neatly kept.

Tom Wallington, who was born 1889, lived at Lawn Farm,
near Wotton Underwood for thirty years, and recalls that they
made quite a lot of use of Wood Siding, where they used to
take milk every day. Other farmers from Piddington and
Ludgershall did the same. This was before the building of the
GWR station at the latter village. At that time, the man in
charge was Alfred Roberts, who lived in the isolated group of
cottages nearby called Waterloo Cottages. His place was taken
in about 1913 by another man, Benny Witchert, who lived at
Brill. Benny seemed to enjoy his isolated post at the little
station, with just a small hut and an occasional visit from a
passing farmer livening his day between trains. Then there was
always the sudden rush and great palls of white smoke as the
mighty Great Western engine thundered, unseen, beneath. It
was an otherwise tranquil spot for a working railwayman but the
isolation would not have suited many.

Mrs Young has a very special reason for her personal regard
for the old Tramway, as she was born in the first cottage of
the group at Brill Station. Her father was clerk-in-charge at
Brill Station until his tragically early death, on 13th February
1904, from consumption. His name was Thomas Wilkins, and
he began his employment on the Tramway in 1881 as a guard.
He had moved from the village of Gawcott, near Buckingham,
for this employment. Mrs Young reflected, sadly, that his
long hours exposed in the variable climate had aggravated his
chronic condition beyond medication, by the time that promotion brought the shelter of a warm office and a little extra
comfort.

On her mother's side, Mrs Young was related to the
Varneys, some of whom also served on the Tramway, although
Alfred Varney was working in the field alongside the line on a
farm machine when tragedy struck him. The field was somewhere between the 'black tank' and Thame Lodge, where he
had stopped to make some adjustments to the machine, immediately alongside the track. He paid no particular attention to the
approach of the Manning Wardle engine, but unfortunately it
startled the horse which moved forward and pulled the machine
over Varney's head; he was killed instantly.

A Mrs Rowley of Weston Turnville originally came from
Waddesdon, where her father worked on the Rothschild Estate.
Her recollections, vividly clear, are of particular interest concerning the Kingswood branch, about which precious little is
known. She remembered the little house at the end where the
coalman, Mr Crook, lived, and the heaps of coal alongside the
line. But it is with regard to the little Wotton Underwood Brick
& Tile Works that her memory sheds interesting light. The kiln
of the works looked like a small tunnel, with the bricks stacked
inside and then sealed up. The bricks were moved around the
small yard in trucks, similar to the kind used in coal mines.

Brill No. 1 at Brill with, left to right, Jack Lewis and 'Slasher' Horne, who worked at Brill early in his railway career but went on to the footplate on the Metropolitan at Neasden. The horse whip is in the hand of Jack Shipperley, who operated a carrier business from the station. Porter Tom Cook is beside him with the indestructible Harry Cross displaying his engine from the steps.

Mike Crosbie

Wotton House, the home of the Dukes of Buckingham and the Earls Temple.

Bill George

The only person known in this well-dressed group on the platform at Brill is the man with the flower in his buttonhole, and the raincoat over his arm. This is Fred Axtell, one of the village postmen, who was a very keen and competitive horticulturalist. Perhaps they are preparing to go on a Sunday trip in the coach to be hauled by No. 23. The old Wotton Tramway trains shed survives well, still in use as the goods shed.

Roy Slaymaker

A section of the early bridge rail, with decomposition of the bearing surface, possibly a residual effect of compression.
Author's Collection/Courtesy Quainton Railway Preservation Society

Within ten miles of its original location, Wood Siding Station building, as a garden shed.

Author's Collection

When it was time to clear the yard of the build-up of bricks, the men, dressed in overalls that buttoned straight up to the neck, with caps fitted with ear muffs, would lay down a sectional railway along the road up to the railhead. Each section could easily be handled by one man as they were put in place and then bolted together. As soon as this was accomplished, they would pull and shove two loaded trucks at a time up the line to the waiting railway wagons. When the yard had been cleared of bricks, the men would dismantle their unpermanent way and store it in the yard until the next shipment had been built-up. The memory of this procedure is so clear in Mrs Rowley's mind, that she remembers that the men would allow them to ride back in the empty trucks from the railhead. The men themselves would stand on the backs of the trucks riding along also on the roll of gravity.

Her other recollections include a time, in 1916, when the driver of the Manning Wardle engine stopped the train to let them walk across a nearby field to see a strange contraption called an aeroplane which had landed in a field near the line.

With regard to the character types working on the line, one man stands out for his ribaldry and daring sense of humour. This was Harry Cross, who appears on a number of photographs. Harry's ready smile and carefree nature did, on a num-

ber of occasions, lead him astray. Originally, he worked for the London & North Western Railway, and his departure from the services of that company proved to be something of a wry coincidence in view of his predilection for sampling the beverage of the Swan Inn, Brill, even when on duty; for his departure was the result of running his engine into the back of a beer train. With similar exuberance, he removed the back of Brill engine shed, on two occasions, and laid claim to be the only employee on the Metropolitan Railway that had knocked down every crossing gate. Notwithstanding Harry's cheery wave leaning over the engine at every station, and his sojourn in the Railway Arms at Quainton, no one ever came to any harm from his indelicacy with timber structures, and his companionable nature is regarded with much warmth from people that remember him. The Swan Inn at Brill was closed during World War II.

At about the same time as Harry Cross, was Jack Lewis, who also appears on photographs. Jack came to Brill Station after being a driver on the Metropolitan Railway. Unfortunately, he met with a bad accident when his engine struck a loose piece of rail which spun up from the track and punctured the boiler; this caused him some very bad scalding. He never returned to the footplate, but worked the rest of his railway career, until retire-

Wotton Stables, twenty years after closure.

John Pritchett Collection

ment, on the staff of Brill Station.

Of the footplate staff, none are now alive. Fortunately, something of the Aylesbury to Verney Junction line can still be recollected by ex-Metropolitan driver, Bill Fry, who still lives near Neasden. To begin with, he remembers a journey down the Tramway. 'One of the A class engines, No. 27, came off the road at the points of Wotton Station siding in 1930, we took another A class together with the breakdown vans, but it was found to be quite a simple matter to put the engine bogies back on the track by using wedges. If they had had wedges, the men on the engine could have done it themselves, but this would have been strictly against regulations, as whenever an engine came off the track it had to be reported to Neasden for assistance immediately; it was a bumpy old road, that Brill line. At Aylesbury Shed, in 1912, we had two GWR locomotives of the 22 class and two 35 class; one of the latter was painted a chocolate colour. This was used for the push-pull train to Princes Risborough in the early morning, and then spent its day working between Princes Risborough and Banbury. In the evening, it would work a train back to its own shed at Aylesbury. A method used to fill the header water tank at Aylesbury was to attach a pipe to the whistle valve on the

engine, which would operate a pulseometer (water pump). There was a small furnace in the shed for drying sand and to help with lighting up. There was also an office and store. The engine in the picture (*see page 101*) is on the GWR road. There was also an office for the Metropolitan Railway. The new water tank in the picture appears to be directly over the original well that was used. Metropolitan engines on the shed were one F class, one D class Brill engine, and a Manning Wardle which was still being used up until 1914. The F class worked the goods to Verney at 3 o'clock in the morning and then worked back again to Aylesbury with what was usually a 400 ton goods, after the extensive marshalling and deployment of wagons at Verney. In my recollection, the end of the shed at Aylesbury was a brick wall and not through-running. The Great Central also kept four engines at Aylesbury.

'Aylesbury had a rudimentary coaling stage beneath the water tank, and a simple crane would lift ½ ton tubs of coal off for the GCR locomotives but the Metropolitan and GWR used 2cwt. baskets'.

'Staff was kept distinctly separate, and the GWR had four engine crews and five cleaners with a general hand fitter. The Metropolitan also had four crews and one general hand

The Ashbury coach as permanent way men's hut at Brill in October 1935. Further use of bridge rail, still on baulks, is supporting it.

S. W. Baker

Wotton Station bustles with activity on the final day, with a two coach train.

The late G. K. J. Kerley

Activity in steam from *Coventry No. 1* at the Brill branch platform at Quainton Road in 1980.

Author's Collection

fitter. The GCR had four crews, five cleaners and one man in charge. The F class engine, No. 92, worked up to Harrow with the goods whilst the notorious D class, which tended to be unsteady, could blow-back even with the blower on hard. However, they were useful on goods trains, especially Nos. 74, 75 and 76 which had larger boilers. A regular turn for them was the No. 8 goods at Aylesbury'.

'Worst running between Aylesbury and Verney Junction was a section between Quainton and Grandborough called Hogshaw Bank, a gradient of 1 in 600. When the Verney goods trains started to make 600 tons, it was decided to send K class engines to work them. Often, there were heavy cattle specials worked to and from both Granborough Road and Quainton. Verney Junction also held large coal shipments for bringing down the Metropolitan line, brought to that point by the L&NWR. Also, a great deal of shop merchandise was carried. This was in fitted trains of box vans, brought up from Farringdon on the electricity to Neasden then from there to Aylesbury by G class engines, which did rather poorly on passenger work but put up a good performance on goods work, almost as good as the Ks.

'Travel on the Metropolitan Pullman was 1s. 6d. (7½p)

above the normal first class fare, and each night the car was kept in the siding just south of Aylesbury Station. There was some special traffic in 1914, with trains bringing a great deal of material for Wendover Camp down from Verney Junction.'

'A word on the system of management of the 'Joint'. This was controlled in five yearly cycles between the Metropolitan and GCR. This made it possible to be promoted up through either company depending whoever was in charge when one was serving on the line.'

Bill ended on a personal note by mentioning Bill Newton, who was the last 'passed' fireman on the Brill line. 'Before he went there he was mortified when the post became vacant at Brill in 1928, as he was hoping to attain better things and stay in the link at Neasden. He tried to find a person to change with him but no one wanted to be despatched to this lonely self-contained outpost of the Metropolitan, so Bill had to go. A few years later, no one could find a happier man, for he married a local girl and lived out an almost paradisiacal existence on the little line, well away from the gaffers. Doubtless, it was as great a regret, or possibly greater, when he found that he had to give up his little kingdom in 1935 upon closure'.

Bill George of Grendon Underwood, in addition to serving

on various committees, is also a member of the Aylesbury Vale District Council. Within his great passion for the Great Central Railway, he has an abiding fondness for the old Tramway that he remembers quite distinctly. He remembers, in 1929, the man in charge at Waddesdon had a delicate little crystal set, which he used to attach with an ariel to the station telegraph pole. Ears straining, he would listen carefully for the afternoon's horse racing results, then telegraph them to no less attentive ears all down the line to Brill. The same man would have his attention quickly aroused by a runaway van carrying a large piece of the crossing gates between Waddesdon and Quainton on its buffer beam down the line towards him. Luckily, the runaway rolled to a stop before ascending the slight incline to his station, and progressed more slowly back to whence it came. Obviously, something had gone seriously amiss at Quainton!

Twenty years after the Brill line closed, and only a few years before the closure of Quainton Road Station, during the 1950s, Jack Turner, a fireman on the Midland Region of British Railways, recounts his days working in this corner of Buckinghamshire.

'For many years Aylesbury engine shed had been a Metropolitan/GCR and GWR Joint depot, before it became part of the Midland Region. Therefore there remained two links of men; the general link and a Metropolitan link. The Metropolitan link still had two old Metropolitan drivers in it, Archie Keating and Bert Coles. They covered the Aylesbury to Baker Street trains, and goods trains from Quainton Road to Harrow and Neasden. Having these two drivers meant that no goods trains originating from the Metropolitan route (Neasden, Harrow, Rickmansworth, Aylesbury) went beyond Quainton Road. All goods traffic was exchanged there, with the services from Woodford and Bletchley. One of the turns that I covered as a fireman, on rest day cover, was the overnight Harrow empties, which worked forward from Aylesbury at 03.40. All that we did was to back them into the 'down' sidings at Quainton Road and, after uncoupling, draw forward with light engine on to the old Brill Tramway lines, now part of the 'down' sidings. Our engine for this duty was, at first, one of the ex-GCR A5 4-6-2 tanks; later we had an LMS/BR(4) 3000 class 4F4P 2-6-0. There, in the absolute still of open country, we simmered for nearly four hours as the dawn light broke into the cab. Suddenly, the silence would be broken by the clear exhaust echoes of an ex-GCR J11 0-6-0, or sometimes, quite spectacularly, by an ex-GCR O4 ROD 2-8-0, with the 6.40a.m. household coal train from Woodford. After he had placed this into the 'up' siding, he would cross over to pick up the empties that we had brought, and take them back to Woodford. Things were livening up by now, for not long after he had disappeared, a Bletchley 8F 2-8-0 would come pounding into view to pick up other empties that had been left in the sidings during the previous day. Having completed his task, he would follow in the path of the previous train leaving us to cross over and collect the household coal, which we would shunt in required train formation. This would then constitute the 'up' goods back to Aylesbury and on to Harrow.'

'Our jobs in the general link would take us beyond Quainton Road to Woodford and Bletchley with passenger and parcel trains. Another job that would take us to Banbury was the working of the ex-GWR auto-train from Princes Risborough, with a 14XX class, usually No. 1473; this was kept at Aylesbury Shed.'

Jack's interesting recollection, which recalls train working in the district over thirty years ago, in the age of steam locomotives, brings this final chapter and history to a close. Quainton, nowdays, sees the occasional Class 25 diesel on the Calvert 'Landfill' train, whilst locomotive-hauled parcel trains pass along the main line and across the Claydon spur to reach Rugby on the West Coast Main Line. Diesel multiple unit specials, and overhaul rakes bound for Wolverton also pass through and, as previously mentioned, it is thankfully preserved. Perhaps one might, for a moment, be allowed an imaginative whiff of sheer indulgence that, by some magical philanthropy, a set of rails were laid down as far as Waddesdon Road Station and No. 23 came out of retirement to run once more the hedgerow railway, alongside the road to Quainton village.

Lad Porter, Leslie H. Harding, seventeen years old, photographed not long after he began his railway career on the Brill line at Westcott Station on 26th March 1926. With promotion at nineteen to signalman, Leslie went to work on the Aylesbury to Verney Junction section, in Grandborough Road and Winslow Road boxes. Two photographs that he took of these boxes, exterior and interior, are included in this book. When the line closed he went to work at Aylesbury. Amongst his remarkable recollections is seeing the Directors' saloon hauled up the Brill line and back from Quainton Road by Metropolitan H class engine No. 108, circa 1928. Also during his time at Westcott, he witnessed two Great Western coaches stored in the short siding for the officers of the 3rd Battalion of The Grenadier Guards, who were on manoeuvres in Coopers Field, alongside the gasworks. Remarkably, when he was in his early railway years, his father told him that the contractor's siding from the Brill line to the building of Waddesdon Manor did, in fact, connect with the Tramway in the yard at Waddesdon Station, and crossed Akeman Street Road before ascending Lodge Hill.

L. H. Harding

Detail of Brill Station building during the late 1920s. The Metropolitan Railway extols the delights of the large department stores in London, on its 'Summer Shopping' poster. Such a gregarious enticement would be more likely to bemuse than disaffect the shopping routine of Brill village. Alongside it, the Great Central Railway board prosaically states the LNER timetable. Remote from the regions of Cumbria, a Furness Railway wagon, piled with large pieces of stone, is intriguingly tucked alongside the goods shed. The questioning peep of two cloth-capped 'Jackie Coogan' characters, from behind the building, reflects the kind of personal interest that made this line unique amongst a few.

Ken Benest Collection

MIXED TRAINS, CHESHAM AND BRILL BRANCHES.

Goods Wagons not fitted with the Continuous Brake or through pipe may only be conveyed by Trains carrying passengers on the Brill Branch or on the Chesham Branch in those cases where, in the current Working Time Table, such Trains are shown as conveying goods, except in cases of urgency, when one goods or cattle wagon only may be conveyed behind the rear van of local Passenger Trains on such sections of the line as the Committee's Regulations permit the running of vehicles behind the rear brake van.

The Engine, Tender, and Passenger Vehicles of all Mixed Trains must be provided with the Continuous Brake worked from the Engine, and Goods Wagons attached thereto must be placed behind the rear brake of the Passenger Coaches, with a brake van in the rear of the wagons, in which a Guard must ride. This does not apply to the Brill Branch, where the wagons are attached next the Engine and the continuous brake is not used on any part of the train.

No Mixed Train must exceed 13 Vehicles (excluding Engine), including 3 Passenger Coaches and 9 Goods Wagons and Brake. The maximum of 10 Goods Vehicles must never be exceeded.

Drivers of Mixed Trains must not exceed a speed of **25 miles an hour.**

BRILL BRANCH.

The Engineman must have his Engine and Train **well under control in descending all inclines, especially those on the Quainton straight road, at Blue Bottle, and between Brill and Wotton, and on commencing to descend these inclines he should not require to put on the Engine brake, but sufficient power must be put down by the Guard in the Train to keep the Train back from pressing on the Engine, the Engine brake being reserved for any emergency.**

The speed must not exceed 25 miles per hour, reduced at level crossings to 8 miles per hour, and at Lodge Level Crossing to 4 miles per hour.

A view from the engine, as the guard opens the level crossing gates at the crossing near to Quainton Station on 12th October 1935.

S. W. Baker

LEVEL CROSSING GATES, BRILL BRANCH.

Referring to General Rule No. 118, which provides for all level crossing gates being kept normally closed across the highway. all crossing gates (except that at Wotton Lodge) on the Brill Branch are exempted from the operation of this rule, and are normally kept closed across the railway.

At Wotton Lodge the gates are normally closed across the highway. These gates open on to the highway.

At Quainton level crossing, the fireman of the Brill Branch train will open the gates for the passing of the train, and close them after it has passed.

In order to warn Drivers of their approach to the Quainton Road Gates during foggy weather or snow storms the Station Master at **QUAINTON ROAD must arrange for one Detonator to be placed on the rails a quarter of a mile on the Brill side of the gates at least 15 minutes before each Up Train is due at Quainton Road.**

The scene between Thame Lodge and Wood Siding.

London Transport Executive